Design for Learning

This important book is the result of a study of school curriculum undertaken by a joint committee of the University of Toronto and the Board of Education for the City of Toronto. Three sub-committees, dealing with English, Social Science, and Physical Science, here present preliminary reports which indicate the need for perpetual study if the school curriculum is to be kept abreast of modern developments in each discipline.

Committee members responsible for the reports are themselves elementary, secondary or university teachers of experience. Their recommendations, embracing all grades up to and including Thirteen, are specific, stimulating and controversial. They are unanimous only in their concern that necessary changes be made and that study of the curriculum be continuous and objective.

The reports are prefaced by a discerning essay written by Northrop Frye, Principal of Victoria College, University of Toronto. Commenting on the unique nature of this curriculum study, Principal Frye points out that "the real barriers to break down were those between the three major divisions of education, the primary, secondary and university levels, each of which tends to become a self-enclosed system, congratulating itself on its virtues and blaming whatever deficiencies the educational process as a whole may have on the other systems."

This book will be of interest to teachers at all levels, to officials responsible for policy in our public education, to trustees, to parents, and to the increasing number of the general public who care about education.

The Chairmen of the three sub-committees were: English, Mary Campbell (Parkdale Collegiate Institute); Social Science, C. B. Macpherson (Department of Political Economy, University of Toronto); Physical Science, Charlotte M. Sullivan (Department of Zoology, University of Toronto). The Editor, Northrop Frye, is Principal of Victoria College, University of Toronto.

DESIGN FOR LEARNING

Reports submitted to the

Joint Committee of the

Toronto Board of Education

and the University of Toronto

Edited

with an Introduction by

NORTHROP FRYE

University of Toronto Press

Preface

The University of Toronto and the Board of Education for the City of Toronto were both established in 1850, and in a geographic sense the two institutions have always been closely associated. The building of the Board's Education Centre on College Street ensures that this association will long continue.

But until the establishment in November 1960 of a Joint University–Board Committee there has never been a formal relationship between the two institutions. Discussions of educational problems have always been carried on between members of the two staffs but almost always on an unofficial basis and never in a long-continued and systematic manner. The creation of a Joint Committee, five members to be nominated by the President of the University of Toronto and five by the Chairman of the Toronto Board of Education, is an attempt to make the association of the two institutions as functional as it is geographically convenient.

The first action of the Joint Committee was the appointment of five subcommittees in the major areas of the curriculum: English, Foreign Languages, Mathematics, Science, and Social Sciences, each committee including representatives from the elementary school, the secondary school, and the university. A generous grant of $15,000 from the Atkinson Charitable Foundation enabled some members of three of these subcommittees to work full-time for one month during the summer of 1961 on the question of curriculum reform in their area. The reports prepared by these three committees were submitted to the Joint Committee in November 1961. Though individual members of the Joint Committee were far from prepared to agree with all the conclusions of all the reports, there was unanimous agreement that the reports were of considerable significance and deserved wide circulation. Hence the decision to publish them in this volume, together with an introduction by Principal Northrop Frye. The Joint Committee regards Principal Frye's essay as the first speech in what is hoped will be an extensive debate on a fascinating and urgent problem.

ROBIN S. HARRIS

ROY C. SHARP

Co-chairmen Joint Committee

A NOTE ON THE ORGANIZATION OF EDUCATION IN ONTARIO

Since the three committee reports are based on the course of study adopted in the Province of Ontario, they assume familiarity with the organization of education in that province. From the standpoint of curriculum, the basic facts are these.

Children are required to attend school from the ages of 6 to 16. Responsibility for the provision of schools and the hiring of teachers is vested in local boards of education elected by ratepayers, but responsibility for the curriculum rests with the Provincial Department of Education, headed by a Minister of Education, who is an elected member of the Legislature. Elementary schooling extends from Grade 1 to Grade 8, secondary schooling from Grade 9 to Grade 13. A Secondary School Graduation Diploma (Junior Matriculation) is granted on the successful completion of Grade 12, the final examinations being set and marked by the staff of the local secondary school. An Honour Secondary School Graduation Diploma (Senior Matriculation) is granted to the student who obtains standing in eight subjects (English Cmposition and English Literature are required) at the Senior Matriculation examinations conducted by the Department of Education in June of each year; these are external examinations which are set and marked by committees on which the universities are well represented. However, the Honour Graduation Diploma is in itself not valid for university entrance. Most universities in Ontario require a standing of at least 60 per cent in nine Grade 13 papers, including two in English and two in a second language.

Contents

Contributors

ENGLISH

MARY A. CAMPBELL (*Chairman*), Head of English Department, Parkdale Collegiate Institute

ROBERT P. MCDONALD, Head of English Department, Oakwood Collegiate Institute

J. EDWARD PARSONS, Teacher of English, Clinton Street Public School

A. DOUGLAS SPARKS, Vice-Principal, Deer Park Public School

DONALD F. THEALL, Associate Professor, Department of English, St. Michael's College

SOCIAL SCIENCES

C. B. MACPHERSON (*Chairman*), Professor, Department of Political Economy, University of Toronto

EVAN CRUIKSHANK, Teacher of History, Humberside Collegiate Institute

H. I. NELSON, Assistant Professor, Department of History, University of Toronto

LLOYD A. DENNIS, Principal, Deer Park Public School

WILLIAM SAGER, Assistant Professor (Methods in Geography), Ontario College of Education

JOHN SAYWELL, Assistant Professor, Department of History, University of Toronto

SCIENCE

CHARLOTTE M. SULLIVAN (*Chairman*), Associate Professor, Department of Zoology, University of Toronto

A. D. ALLEN, Associate Professor, Department of Chemistry, University of Toronto

ROBERT W. MCKAY, Associate Professor, Department of Physics, University of Toronto

D. G. IVEY, Associate Professor, Department of Physics, University of Toronto

GEORGE BAKER, Vice-Principal, Queen Alexandra Public School (now on leave of absence)

GRANT G. HERN, Head of Chemistry and Biology Department, Parkdale Collegiate Institute

LESLIE A. SMITH, Head of Chemistry and Biology Department, Harbord Collegiate Institute

JOHN S. WRIGHT, Head of Physics Department, Oakwood Collegiate Institute

Design for Learning

Introduction

NORTHROP FRYE

Near the beginning of 1960, some trustees and officials of the Toronto Board of Education approached a number of professors and administrators in the University of Toronto, including the present writer, to discuss problems of common interest. A loosely organized *ad hoc* committee began to meet during the summer, talking somewhat at random in the hope of defining a central question. There were several things that caused us some concern: the number of students not finishing high school, the number of able students not reaching university; the number of secondary school graduates unable to adjust to university methods of work; the role of Grade 13 in the transitional process; and so on. But for the most part we were merely following the mysterious law which says that no society can flourish, or in the modern world even survive, until it learns never to let well enough alone. Even so, we were a little surprised to discover what our central question was. It turned out to be an academic question: does teaching in the schools, or at least the secondary schools, reflect contemporary conceptions of the subjects being taught? The answer was no. Changes of perspective have taken place in all fields of knowledge which teachers outside the university find great difficulty in keeping up with, and even greater difficulty in applying to their present curricula. Before we began to meet, refresher courses had been started for teachers in history and science, but these could go only so far. There was no question of the school curriculum being false in its philosophy or dangerous in its social effects; but a synoptic survey of it, in contemporary terms, did seem to be called for.

The non-university members of the committee pointed out that in front of the theoretical question lay a practical one. Does not the university have a heavy responsibility in the larger educational process? The university, unlike the schools, has the resources for keeping up with advances in scholarship, and hence has some obligation to make its knowledge socially effective. The University of Toronto has always assumed (correctly in this writer's opinion) that "education" as an academic subject has no place in a liberal-arts undergraduate programme, and belongs to postgraduate professional training. But there is some danger that the university may withdraw too far from other educational operations. A professor is not doing all he can do to maintain educational standards merely by cursing the secondary schools for not sending him better prepared students. Perhaps he knows nothing about secondary school curricula, much less anything about the difficulties or the positive achievements of the secondary schools. Perhaps he can't teach, and so has no sense of proportion about what a good preparation would be. Perhaps he is not making a first-rate job himself of training those of his students who are going to be secondary-school teachers. As all the latter have to pass through the university, the university ought to be fully aware of its own educational context.

The university members of the committee of course admitted all this, and we felt that we were beginning to get somewhere. This was, so far as I know, the first time in Toronto's history that the University and the Board of Education had really talked to each other about education. (We have since gathered that such meetings are extremely rare in North American cities generally.) Clearly there was some value in breaking down barriers. But of course the real barriers to break down were those between the three major divisions of education, the elementary, secondary, and university levels, each of which tends to become a self-enclosed system, congratulating itself on its virtues and blaming whatever deficiencies the educational process as a whole may have on the other systems. How could we get these together? We discussed the possibility of a conference. But obviously any conference would have to have a great deal of preparatory work done for it if it were to reach any conclusions likely to impress the public. Eventually we began to see that it was this preparatory work which it was our business to organize.

So our *ad hoc* committee sought and obtained the blessing of the Board and the University, was formally constituted a Joint Committee and, after some changes in personnel, settled down to become a steering committee for a group of study committees of teachers. Five of these were set up, in English, foreign languages, mathematics, science and social science, each with representatives from the Toronto elementary and secondary schools, and the University of Toronto. After four or five meetings they brought in preliminary reports which while brief indicated that full-time work might produce unusually interesting results. A grant from the Atkinson Charitable Foundation made it possible to finance a full month's work for three of them, the committees in English, Science and Social Sciences. Once the steering committee had decided on its proper strategy, its tactics became very simple. What we had to do was to get the best teachers we could find and then leave them alone. The three committees worked hard and long during the summer of 1961, and their reports are the substance of this book.

Obviously we need corresponding surveys in mathematics and in non-English languages, perhaps, too, in art, music and other subjects. But even without them we now have the outlines of a survey telling us a good deal about the gap, which exists in teaching as in all areas of human effort, between stated objective and actual achievement. It is easy enough to formulate the most admirable statements of aims in education ("All the ones we have seen are very nice," the Social Science report remarks dryly), and such statements enable us to see what is being done in our classrooms in some kind of perspective. There remains the question of whether the statement of aims is realistic or not, and this is connected with the state of scholarship contemporary with the subjects being taught. In reading through the English report, the only one of the three that I can comment on with any technical assurance, I was struck by the fact that when the authors ran into a difficulty, the difficulty was usually caused by a defect in contemporary critical theory. It looked as though there should be some regular means by which the teaching programme could be re-examined continuously in the light of advances in scholarship.

So on the horizon of our immediate problem there loomed a much larger task, the outlines of which only gradually took shape. This we are now able to describe as a kind of institute of curricular research, a permanent centre where scholars and teachers are engaged in working out the implications for teaching, at all levels, of improvements in scholarship in the subjects being taught. The axiom underlying its activity would be that the ability to explain the elementary principles of a subject to children is the only real guarantee that the subject itself is theoretically coherent. The physical sciences are theoretically coherent by this test at present; literature and the social sciences much less so.

II

These reports are academic in the sense in which academics themselves use that term. They do not represent any educational pressure group or interest. They are not aimed at the Provincial Department with a view to influencing its policy; they are addressed to the informed public, and discuss the kind of thing that might be done. The Department has two observers on the steering committee, and is interested in and sympathetic towards the work presented here, but obviously the relationship cannot be more official than that at this stage. The reports have been approved in principle by the steering committee, but not without sharp expressions of specific disagreement from some members of that committee. They do not in fact wholly agree with one another, though there is an underlying unity to them which it is the purpose of the present introduction to elucidate. If the reader also finds himself disagreeing with them, he will learn something from his disagreement that he would not learn by compulsory agreement with a mass of platitudes. They have not been written in committee jargon, but in lucid, often brilliant, prose; they are designed to be read, and read with an active and critical response. They are, in short, a candid, independent, disinterested fresh look at what we are trying to do in our education.

The authors are teachers, unfamiliar with the typical stalling devices of educational bureaucrats. One of the commonest of these is the plea that no theory of education will be of any use until we have a statistically, psychologically and neurologically irrefutable theory of the child's learning processes. This subject in itself is certainly important enough: the steering committee has two advisers who are experts in this field, one attached to the University and the other to the Board. But, as all the reports clearly indicate, one of the essential data for research into the child's learning processes is an intelligible programme for teaching him, and every improvement in the latter changes the situation of the former. Further, the authors are good teachers, and consequently have none of the maudlin enthusiasm for the "inspired" teacher which assumes that an inspired teacher of, say, mathematics can get inspired by something which is not mathematics. What inspires a good teacher is a clarified view of his own subject. There will always be average teachers as well as average students, and what inspires a good teacher will at least help an average one. The Social Science report observes that the criteria of adequacy are the same for students going on and not going on to university: "What is good for one group is good for the other" (page 81). The English report asks: "Is not what these young people have in common as human beings more important and more relevant than their differences?" (page 36). But these things can only be true when excellence sets the standard for mediocrity, for in education, as in religion, we may be inspired by a vision of something that we cannot reach. If mediocrity becomes a kind of censor principle setting the standard for excellence, all teachers and students at all levels suffer alike.

Because the authors are writing as teachers and not as educators, their approach is pragmatic. Nevertheless one can see the reflection in them of a considerable change of emphasis in recent educational theory. This change of emphasis is something very different from what is discussed in newspapers and in popular rumour. The learned have their demonologies no less than the unlearned, and the bogey of the "progressive" educator, with his incessant straw-threshing of "teaching methods," his fanatical hatred of the intellect, and his serene conviction that everyone who is contemptuous of his maunderings must be devoted to the dunce cap and the birch rod, still haunts university classrooms. He does in fact still exist, though educators today pay him little attention and no respect. Never, perhaps, a major threat to Ontario schools, his incompetence elsewhere helped to create the power vacuum which has done much to make education more subject to political interference than the other professions. The Canadian aspect of this problem has been discussed by Frank MacKinnon in *The Politics of Education* (University of Toronto Press, 1960). The kind of vague panic which urges the study of science and foreign languages in order to get to the moon or to uncommitted nations ahead of the Communists is equally remote from the educational issues that these reports face. Human nature being what it is, serious educators would probably not have got as much public support for their efforts without headlines about sputniks, but they could see the facts of the situation without benefit of such headlines. I recently talked to a supervisor of curriculum in an American public school who told me that he had been sent a science text-book for elementary grades, from a usually reliable publisher, which he had rejected out of hand, on the ground that it contained no science. I was gratified to hear this, but ventured to suggest that he might not have thought it a real objection to the book a few years ago. He said: "No, but we're teaching stuff in third grade now that we didn't use to touch until junior high." Hence books containing only advice on what to do if one's playmate turns anti-social, and the like, can no longer be used for "science" text-books. This was not Ontario, but Ontario is bound to be affected by the eroding or shoring up of educational standards elsewhere.

The assumption in all these reports is that the school and the teacher, *qua* school and teacher, have no other function than an educational one. Hence the aim of whatever is introduced into the school curriculum, at any level, should be educational in the strict and specific sense of that word. It was the confusion of educational and social functions, implicit in the motto, "The whole child goes to school," that made "progressive" theories so fatuous. The axiom that the entire school programme should be specifically educational leads naturally to questions of proportion and distribution, or of what may be called the economy of education. How much science, social science, and English is appropriate at each year of training? What is the point at which repetition ceases to be a means of sound learning and becomes discouraging and sterile (cf. page 95)? Another problem, outside the scope of these reports, is that of priorities.

Which are the basic disciplines at each level, and how can we decide between the claims of two subjects competing for the same place in the timetable? We need additional reports for these questions, as it is particularly the tendency to push foreign languages further back into elementary schools that is likely to cause traffic jams in the near future. Many of the problems of the rhythm of education, which should be that of a leisurely progress, a golden mean between dawdling and cramming, cannot be solved by theory but only by the tactics of the classroom. Yet there are questions of theory which strike their roots deeply into the structure of the subjects taught and into the nature of democratic society.

From the beginning, the study committees were interested in the remarkable success of the Woods Hole Conference of 1959 in the United States, and in the book by Jerome Bruner, *The Process of Education* (Harvard University Press, 1960), which consolidated the results of its findings. Dr. Bruner was invited from Harvard to visit and address the committees in February of 1961, and it was he who suggested the idea of an institute of curricular research (already alluded to). The Woods Hole conceptions of a "spiral curriculum" and the prime importance of structure in elementary teaching have entered deeply into all the reports (cf. page 22). These conceptions are, as we should expect, new only in context; inherently they are very old conceptions, but they have to be revived in a new form with every generation.

It is doubtless true, as Bruner says, that the original thinker pushing back the frontier of knowledge and the child confronting a major conception for the first time are psychologically in very similar positions. But they are not in the same context of the subject itself. The original thinker is probably (almost certainly if he is a scientist) proceeding inductively, making new experiments in a new conceptual area and drawing new conclusions from them. Once his conclusions become established, the procedure for everyone who follows him and repeats his experiments becomes deductive. The theory comes first and the experiments test it, and at last, when the theory is fully established, simply illustrate it. It follows that elementary teaching is naturally of a strongly deductive cast. Once this is realized, a great deal of time can be saved, and a great many random observations and experiences may become examples of central principles. The conception of the subject to be taught should therefore be, not a conception of content, or of so much information to be "covered," but a conception of structure.

The Science report is particularly careful and successful in explaining how genuinely scientific principles can be introduced to the youngest children when made sufficiently simple and concrete, and in showing that they are no more difficult to comprehend than non-scientific or pseudo-scientific activities like washing woollens or feeding pets (page 123). We are thus led to the startling but quite logical conclusion that children six years old can, and should, be studying physics, chemistry and biology, presentations of which can be made intelligible to the six-year-old mind. Such principles as energy can be illustrated by almost everything a child does, and the fact that he gets warmer when he runs may introduce him to laws of thermodynamics and the principle of entropy (page 147). As the child's mind develops from the sensational to the conceptual, the things he understands unconsciously, such as how to calculate the speed and trajectory of a ball thrown at him, become translated into the language of consciousness. Thus we arrive at the principle of a "spiral curriculum" of the same structural elements of a subject being repeated at progressively more complex levels. This principle takes care of the point raised in the Social Science report (page 85) about the need for fresh starts and unlearning as essential in the continuity of the educational process. The English report also urges that the study of English must be literary from the beginning, and that reading texts "too low in vocabulary count, too dully repetitive, too vacuous" (page 27) belong to the outmoded and pernicious scheme of postponing all real education as long as possible.

Increase in complexity of understanding is largely an increase in the capacity of verbalization. This fact gives the English report a more difficult situation to consider than the other two. In the first place, "English" means a literature which is one of the major arts, addressed to the imagination, and in a group with painting and music (pages 58, 73). In the second place, "English" is the mother tongue, the means of understanding and expression in all subjects. The first "English" is chiefly a language of metaphor and analogy; the second is a language of description. These two aspects of English cannot be separated. Mathematics is often said to be the language of science, but it is a secondary language: all elementary understanding of science is verbal, and most of the understanding of it at any level continues to be so. The verbal understanding of science, at least on the elementary level, is quite as much imaginative, quite as dependent on metaphor and analogy, as it is descriptive. Here is a passage from *The Intelligent Man's Guide to Science*, by Isaac Asimov (Basic Books; University of Toronto Press, 1961), which illustrates how metaphorical a writer must become when he has to explain science to scientific illiterates: "Cosmic rays bombarding atoms in the earth's upper atmosphere knock out neutrons when they shatter the atoms; some of these neutrons bounce out of the atmosphere into space; they then decay into protons, and the charged protons are trapped by magnetic lines of force of the earth." This functional use of metaphor is one of the many reasons why no programme of study in English, however utilitarian in its aims, can ever lose contact with English as literature.

In "English" conceived as the language of understanding and description, there is an inductive study of the phenomena of language called linguistics, which is descriptive in its approach, and there is the traditional "grammar," which starts out from a normative position, laying down accepted standards of conventional communication as its premises. One is inductive, the other deductive, in its general direction. The English report shows how completely elementary education in English has to be based on the deductive approach of grammar, at whatever stage its nomenclature needs to be learned. Hence the so-called quarrel of linguists and grammarians, as far as school-teaching is concerned, is a pseudo-problem (page 48).

The structural or deductive pattern in literature is less easy to see, largely because so few contemporary literary critics have reached the point of being able to see it. The authors of the English report get little help from Bruner's book here, beyond a somewhat vague suggestion that tragedy is a central structural principle. As a matter of fact tragedy is one of four modes of literary fiction, the other three being comedy, romance, and irony. Of these, comedy and romance are the primary ones, and can be introduced to the youngest children. Those whose literary tastes do not advance beyond the childish stage never learn to appreciate any form of fiction outside these two modes. Tragedy and irony are more difficult, and belong chiefly to the secondary level. The main line of the argument of the English report on this point is based on the fact that literature is highly conventionalized. The young child can be introduced to the myths, fairy-tales, legends, Bible stories, which are central to our imaginative heritage (pages 28, 30), because all he needs to do to comprehend them is to listen to the story. This is not a passive response, but a kind of imaginative basic training, which those who are continually clutching for meanings and messages in the arts have not learned. As he grows older and his literary experience increases, he begins to realize that there are a limited number of possible ways of telling a story, and that he is already in possession of all of them (page 37). Hence he has, not only a sense of the structure of story-telling implanted in his mind, but a potential critical standard as well, which he badly needs in a world of sub-literary entertainment (page 63).

III

In all learning there is a radical pioneering force and a conservative supporting force, a learning that explores and a learning that consolidates. It seems to me that there are three main phases in the relationship of these two forces, three main turns of the spiral: a primary phase, a secondary phase, and a tertiary phase, which correspond roughly, if not exactly, to the elementary, secondary, and university levels of education.

In the primary phase the consolidating or conservative force is memory. Children seem to have good memories, and many children enjoy the power of using them: like the poets of primitive societies, they have an affinity for catalogues of names, accentual verses, and lists of all kinds that can be delivered in the chanting rhythm of a child's speech. Behind whatever I know of the social and cultural effects of the Norman Conquest is a primitive mnemonic chant of "William the First, William the Second, Henry the First, and *Stee*-phen!" I remember encountering a small girl in California who had just "taken Canada" in school, and who saw in a Canadian visitor an approaching captive audience. She backed me into a corner and recited the names of the provinces of Canada, complete with capitals, quite correctly. A question or two revealed that she had no notion where any of these provinces were. It was unlikely that she had been so badly taught; much more likely that she had simply remembered what interested her, the roll-call of strange names, and tuned out what did not, such as their location in space. Perhaps much the same thing was true of the lad in the Social Science report, with whom I have a good deal of sympathy, who remembered the three voyages of Captain Cook but not the fact that he was an emissary of eighteenth-century British imperialism.

Perhaps in our justified distrust of "mere" memorization we underestimate the power in it that can be harnessed to education. What we are apt to underestimate, in a civilization which is almost compelled to identify education with book-learning, is the role still played in memory by oral and visual experience. Many a boy who cannot remember what countries are in South America can tell the year and make of an automobile a hundred yards away, a feat mainly achieved within what literary critics call the oral tradition. A comic strip recently made an extremely shrewd comment on such extra-curricular learning. Two children in Kindergarten are out for recess; a plane flies overhead; one calls it a jet, the other disagrees, and a quite technical discussion follows on the difference between jet and piston planes. The recess bell rings, and one of them says, "Come on, Mike: we gotta go back and string them beads." What is true of sensational learning is even more obviously true of practical learning, especially in practical skills and sports, where memory develops into motor habit. Elementary science has to be deductively taught, but it does not follow that children should be discouraged from experiment at first hand; and learning to write and to speak intelligible English are practical skills also (page 38, 71). There is a core of truth in the principle of learning by doing, as long as "doing" is not assumed to exclude reading and thinking, and as long as motor activity is not thrust into studies where it has no business to be.

The difference between a good and a mediocre teacher lies mainly in the emphasis the former puts on the exploring part of the mind, the aspects of learning that reveal meanings and lead to further understanding. In English, this means ensuring that a child knows the meaning of what he reads as well as the mechanics of reading; in social and historical studies it means understanding why things happened instead of merely that they happened (page 98); in science it means understanding central principles illustrated by what without them would be a bewildering variety of un-related phenomena (page 140). Unless there is reason and system to give direction to the memory, education burdens the memory; and however resilient a child's memory may be, nobody is going to keep a burden in his mind an instant longer than he is compelled to do. What is merely learned is merely forgotten, as every adult knows. Those who never get psychologically beyond the primary phase of learning are apt to retain a conviction all their lives that total recall is the same thing as intelligence. Until some scandals, which however regrettable were extremely useful to educators, changed the fashion, there was a widespread belief that the "smartest" people were those who proved on television programmes to have the largest stock of information on non-controversial subjects. But it was the sense of how much they themselves had forgotten which gave their audiences a superstitious reverence for those who had been unable to forget.

It is important to realize that the pioneering element in the primary learning process has to do with the reasonable and the systematic, with what makes learning continuous and progressive. It is not a matter of arousing interest or stimulating a student, even to the pitch of enthusiasm. Civilized people respond readily to intellectual stimulation all their lives. Those who speak at business men's luncheons and women's clubs, from pulpits on Sunday morning or through the microphones of the CBC, find intelligent and receptive hearers. But these activities, however valuable in other ways, are not strictly educational. The sense of continuity, of one step leading to another, of details fitting gradually into a larger design, is essential to education, and no sequence of individually isolated experiences can possess this. The fact that all three reports stress the genuinely educational aspect of teaching, rather than the psychologically attractive aspect of it, is one of their most distinctive features. They do not, like so much writing in this field, fail to distinguish between interest and concentration.

Because memory is the more passive element in the learning process, mediocre students tend to rely on their memories, and even good students do so for the subjects in which they are less interested. Mediocre teachers, similarly, and examinations where the marking-schemes have been ossified by a desire to make them mechanically accurate, are also apt to stress memory at the expense of intelligence. Sometimes attempts are made, especially in science, to simplify the grasp of structure into a methodology, but we note that the authors of the Science report, like most scientists, have very little to say about "the scientific method." A scientist enters into the structure of his science, and then uses the same mixture of hunch and common sense that any other mental worker would use. Literature, like mathematics, is practically all structure, and the attempt to master it by memory forces the student to grapple with a pseudo-content, something not really there at all. A teacher who boasted of his ability to get his students through Grade 13 English, would, when teaching Browning's *Epistle* of Karshish, ask his students how many letters Karshish had written (the poem contains the line "And writeth now the twenty-second time"). He admitted that remembering this number was not very central to understanding the poem, but, he argued, unless students had something definite to learn they just gave you a lot of boloney on their examinations. This is the kind of thing I mean by pseudo-content, and its victims are strewn all over the first-year university results in English.

In the secondary phase of learning the pioneering and consolidating forces become more conceptual. The former is now the power of understanding that asks the radical questions: What good is this? How true is it? Could we get along without it? The latter asks the conservative questions: What does this mean? Why is it there? Why has it been accepted? It is particularly in the social sciences that these questions seem relevant, and the Social Science report devotes much attention to them, especially the radical ones. Even with things admitted to be bad, such as slavery or persecution, it is worth asking conservative questions about why the human race has practised them so widely and with such enthusiasm; and even with things admitted to be good, such as religion and democracy, it is worth asking radical questions about what would happen if we did not possess these things, or possessed them in a different form. In literature the student is now advanced enough, not simply to listen to stories, but to inquire within them for real motivation and imaginative causality. Hence his questions here also fall into similar patterns: Why does the author say this? Would this kind of thing really happen? and the like.

Thus the secondary phase of learning revolves around the problem of symbolism. There are realities, and there are appearances related to them. Some appearances represent the reality, as a thermometer represents the temperature or, in a different way, as a drama represents a certain kind of human conflict. Some appearances partly conceal or disguise a reality, like the appearance of the sun "rising" in the east. And some appearances masquerade as reality, like the appearance of lofty intentions in a government about to grab someone else's territory. Learning to sort out these various relationships, or in other words developing what is in the broadest sense a critical intelligence, is the main preoccupation of students on the verge of becoming adult citizens (cf. page 134).

In education properly so called, radical and conservative questions are asked within the subjects themselves. If a student asks, "What use is the conception of gravitation or relativity to physics?" or "What was the point of fighting the Crusades?" or "Why did Shakespeare put a ghost into *Hamlet*?" it is possible to give him a scientific, a historical, and a literary answer respectively. Asking questions about the relation of the subjects themselves to ordinary life is another matter. With young children the educational process competes on fairly even terms with the social one: the young child is interested in everything, and he might as well be interested in his education. But as he gets into his teens the growing power of his social adjustment, where he feels the immediate response of possession, and does not have to be in the humbler position of questioner and seeker, begins to fight against the learning process. This is the stage at which we may see some highly intelligent fourteen-year-old firmly closing his mind to further education, while parents and teachers stand helplessly by, knowing how much he will regret it later on, unable to make the slightest impression on him now. This is the stage too at which many questions are likely to take the form of: "What good is this subject to me when it has no place in the kind of life I now think I want to live?" or "Why should I study science (or history, or literature) when I don't particularly want to study anything?" It is impossible to give a student real answers to such questions, and the weary and helpless answers he does get (e.g., without science we couldn't kill our enemies with bombs or our friends with automobiles) have nothing to do with the actual "good" of these subjects.

We can now see, perhaps, how serious the confusion between social and educational standards, on which the old "progressive" theories foundered, really was. It is because so many intellectually stunted lives result from it that all three reports speak out sharply about every aspect of the confusion that comes to their attention. The Social Science report attacks the "rosy cosy" view of society, of giving a child his own situation (if it *is* his own situation) in the ideal form of a Blakean song of innocence before he has any song of experience to compare it with (page 92). The point is that presenting the child's society to him in the form of a superego symbol is deliberately weighting social standards at the expense of educational ones. The English report says much the same thing about primary readers (page 27), and the Science report insists on the difference between science and technology (page 129), on the impropriety of calling by the name of science the various devices for providing the North American middle class with the comforts of home. I remember a word recognition test given to children in a school which drew from a middle-class group, a lower-middle-class group, and an "under-privileged" group. One of the words was "gown." Children of the first group said a gown was what mummy wore when she went to a party; children of the second group said it was what mummy wore when she went to bed; children of the third group had never heard of the word. Such intrusions of class distinctions into tests of learning and intelligence are not always easy to spot, and may in themselves seem very trifling. But the more fundamental problem of weeding social standards out of educational ones is something that requires constant vigilance and astute criticism. The principle involved is the most important in the whole process of education.

Secondary learning, we suggested, revolves around the relation of appearance and reality. What education as a whole deals with is the reality of human society, the organized forms of intelligence, knowledge and imagination that make man civilized. The middle-class twentieth-century Canadian world the student is living in is the appearance of that society. Education, freedom, and nearly all happiness depend on his not mistaking it for the real form of society. The young student needs to be protected from society, protected by literature against the flood of imaginative trash that pours into him from the mass media, protected by science against a fascination with gadgets and gimmicks, protected by social science against snobbery and complacency. The crisis of his education comes when he is ready to attach himself to the standards represented by his education, detach himself from his society, and live in the latter as a responsible and critical citizen. If he fails to do this, he will remain a prisoner of his society, unable to break its chains of cliché and prejudice, unable to see through its illusions of advertising and slanted news, unable to distinguish its temporary conventions from the laws of God and man, a spiritual totalitarian. Whether he has voluntarily imprisoned himself or whether he has been betrayed by educators under the pretext of adjusting or "orienting" him, he cannot live freely or think freely, but is pinioned like Prometheus on his rock, oriented, occidented, septentrionated, and australized.

The reports do not (except on page 57 ff.) cover university teaching. But the presence of the university, or at least of its liberal-arts undergraduate programme, in the educational process is implied throughout. Each report attempts to outline the programme of study that will be of the greatest value to a student whenever he drops out of it; and they at least imply that the more drive and energy the planning of studies has, the longer the average duration of its appeal to a student is likely to be. The university is concerned specifically with the third phase of learning, where the conservative aspect is the consciousness of the presence of one's own society, with all its assumptions and values, measured against the radical criticism of that society by the standards of accuracy, profundity, and imaginative power to be found in the arts and sciences. The detachment required for this is symbolized in a four-year physical withdrawal from full participation in society. The very small number of university graduates who really achieve such detachment, along with those who achieve it outside the university, are enough to keep our society's head above water. One hardly dares speculate about what might happen if the number were suddenly to increase.

The reports that follow are witty and pointed, sharply critical, and fearless in their expression of criticism. This does not mean that the educational system they discuss is ridiculous or that the authors consider it to be so. They are criticizing something to which they themselves are completely committed. One's vision of life, like the units of one's elementary understanding of science, is a metaphor, and the natural metaphor for any responsible man's job is that of a complex machine, likely to be smashed up in incompetent hands. Contempt for the amateur critic is built into all professions: it is a part of what the late Professor Innis calls the bias of communication. And those who have places of trust in education must often feel, when reading books intended to stir up public resentment, like a farmer seeing his crops trampled and his fences broken by a hunting pack in clamorous pursuit of an enemy that he could have disposed of quickly and quietly with his own shotgun. But these reports have not been written by amateurs, and they are not indictments but specific and sympathetic suggestions. The real power that drives the educational machine, or, in our other image, the final twist on the "spiral curriculum," is the power of self-criticism in teachers, which means the renewing of the vision of the subject they teach. It is such a renewing of vision that is here presented to the public.

REPORT OF THE

English Study Committee

MARY A. CAMPBELL (CHAIRMAN)

R. P. MCDONALD

J. E. PARSONS

A. DOUGLAS SPARKS

DONALD F. THEALL

NOTE. *Mr. A. Douglas Sparks was not able to take part in the Committee's work during the summer of 1961, but wishes to associate himself with the main objectives and recommendations of the report.*

1. INTRODUCTION

Stated in its broadest sense, the purpose of education is to enable man to realize his potentialities as a human being. The development of language is, perhaps, man's most characteristically human achievement. This ordering of sounds to form words and sentences is a miracle of ingenuity, a miracle experienced to some degree anew as small children learn the words and sentence patterns that convey thought and feeling. It is a prime function of the schools to increase the user's power over language, and provide him with keys to the treasures of knowledge, experience, and pleasure that control of language has made possible.

English differs from other subjects in the curriculum in that it is not only a study in itself but a necessity for the understanding of other subjects. In the English-speaking provinces of Canada the ability to speak, read, and write English is a basic requirement before education in the real sense can begin. Without a knowledge of words and the ability to use them in the expression of thought, the learner is crippled. As many reports on education have pointed out, English is inescapably the concern of every teacher.

Education is a continuous process involving activities of many kinds. In language, as in other fields, not all learning takes place in school. All sound formal education, however, presupposes a sense of direction and a goal; teachers with knowledge, discernment, and skill; students able and willing to learn; and materials that nourish both teacher and learner. The origin of this report is the idea of a continuum in education, and of the necessity for making this idea basic in constructing a curriculum. Though a poor teacher can spoil even the best curriculum, it is equally true that an inadequate and unimaginative course of study can limit, and even partially destroy, the work of a good teacher. The committee in English is convinced of the need for an approach that sees the process of education as one of continuous development, and all aspects of the study of English as parts of a whole. The committee does not see cause for alarm in the present state of education in general, or of English studies in particular, but it finds no reason for complacency. It is convinced that, in a period dominated by machines and threatened with destruction, a sense of human identity can be reinforced by making young people more articulate and by revealing for them through literature man's responses to life's infinite variety and complexity.

Committees of teachers and others concerned with the subject of English have met repeatedly to consider its aims, its content, and its teaching methods. For the most part, however, efforts to revise and assess have been made piecemeal, and under severe limitations of time. There have been few attempts to see the subject as a whole, to clarify its relationship with other subjects, and to preserve continuity in its treatment. Investigations have been confined to one stage in education, to the intermediate grades, for example, or Grade 13, or to one aspect of the subject, such as grammar.

Recent developments point to the need for a review of the whole field of English studies. A fresh interest in the principles of learning and in the basic structures of subjects has been noticeable in many recent discussions of education. The value of such an emphasis to English studies should be explored. The Modern Language Association's broad outline of a continuous and sequential programme in English has provoked comment and discussion throughout this continent (*An Articulated English Program*, New York, 1959). It deserves study and experiment. A renewed emphasis on the classical concept of rhetoric as a means of integrating the various parts of the English programme calls for consideration and trial. This approach is discussed in Professor Theall's appendix to the present report. New theories about language study must be assessed, and their application to the work of the classroom must be considered seriously. The claims made for teaching or learning machines should be examined, and teachers and boards informed of the findings.

Professor Jerome Bruner's book, *The Process of Education* (Harvard University Press, 1960), has raised the question of the role of structure in learning. "Grasping the structure of a subject is understanding it in a way that permits many other things to be related to it meaningfully. To learn structure, in short, is to learn how things are related." There follows the suggestion of a spiral curriculum in which the basic principles of a subject would be established early, in simple form, to be revisited at later stages with applications of increasing depth and complexity. Investigation and experiment, Professor Bruner thinks, may discover ways of preventing some of the waste in learning and of presenting greater challenges to the learner.

There is nothing essentially new about the idea of seeking basic principles in the structure of a language, but it is possible that a re-interpretation and extension of the idea to the whole field of English studies might help to provide the synthesis that is needed. The study of literature, of the structure of the language, of words and their associations, and of the art of composition are all aspects of a whole. In practice there is often a fragmentary treatment without controlling principle. The difficulty of defining the scope of the subject is responsible for much confusion and diffusion.

Teaching English requires more than instruction in the elementary skills of reading and writing; it demands training in the comprehension and interpretation of thought, in the structure of sentence and paragraph, in the use of words to convey finite meaning and emotional overtones, in the practice of writing, and in reading with increasing perception of the writer's art. Each facet of the subject raises questions of selection, emphasis, and treatment. The relative importance of speech and writing in our society has been hotly debated, as have different methods of teaching reading. Rigorous training in grammar or the practice of creative writing has been supported by different groups as the solution for problems of expression. The limiting of English studies to the learning of standard usage and the writing of business letters and reports has been advocated as "practical." Literature has sometimes been treated as a form of guidance or of sociology, or interpreted as meaning "dramatics," and writing has been regarded as therapy. Too often ends have been forgotten in the concentration on means. Superficiality on the one hand and minute dissection on the other have damaged the teaching of English.

The subject of English does not lend itself to a rigid or detailed curriculum. Too restrictive a requirement might easily destroy essential values. The object of any course of studies should be to free the teacher to do his best work, not to confine him in a strait jacket. Much of the satisfaction of teaching the subject lies in the opportunities that it gives to the talented, imaginative person to create his own synthesis. But the development of such a synthesis takes years of experience, and classrooms are crowded with inexperienced teachers whose background for the teaching of English is limited. Such teachers need the support of an integrated course of studies to give them a sense of direction.

All teachers of English at all stages should have a general picture of the whole field. Teachers of the early grades do not always realize to what extent they lay the foundations for all future work with language. Teachers of the intermediate grades do not always consider to what extent the work that they do is contributing to a disciplined intelligence. Teachers of the senior grades of secondary schools do not understand how reading has been taught, often fail to acknowledge what has been achieved in the development of language, and sometimes forget to preserve the delight of reading in the emphasis on intensive study of the writer's art. University professors who make general judgments of teaching in the schools on the basis of experience with poorly prepared students do not recognize what their part has been in equipping the teachers, or how harsh judgments may affect the supply of able candidates for the teaching profession.

Parents do not know to what extent their attitude to language and to books can help or hinder learning. Administrators find it difficult to understand why so many complaints reach them about defective English, and why so much time is required for the marking of student writing.

This report assumes that language is everyone's concern. It seeks to indicate some of the principles underlying the study of English, to identify and analyse some of the problems, to suggest some investigations and experiments, and to emphasize the need for *continued* study carried on without haste, and accompanied by test projects with teachers and classes. The report considers the beginning of formal instruction in reading and writing, the teaching of literature, composition, language study, English in Grade 13, English at the university, teacher training, and the impact of the mass media. Following these sections there is a summary of the conclusions reached, and a list of recommendations. The reader will be aware of omissions and repetitions. The first have been caused by limitations of time, or of vision. The repetitions are due to the method of presentation, which appeared to be the most satisfactory under the circumstances.

It may be objected that the report raises questions and expresses doubts, but provides no answers. In accepting the opportunity of making this study, the committee deliberately limited itself to inquiry. A subject so vast as the teaching of English cannot adequately be explored by a small group within a limited period. Such a group can consider general principles, point out problems that require investigation, and make suggestions for further study.

The comments made in this report apply not specifically to Toronto, but to the province of Ontario. Individual members of the committee have been responsible for single sections, but the findings in general have been accepted by the group. The committee's hope is that the report will provide food for reflection, discussion, and action. The greatest regret of the members is that the stimulus of reading, discussion, and interviews on a subject so provocative could not have been shared by more of their colleagues.

2. THE BEGINNING OF FORMAL INSTRUCTION

The child of today is born into a reading and writing world. Never has there been so lively an interest in these two processes as there is now.

Children and books are being brought together through publishers, writers, librarians, and teachers. The whole fabric of a child's educational progress, whether it be slow or rapid, is woven out of the thread of his progress with the written word. Nor is that the sole merit of books. They can bring him enjoyment, supply him with information, satisfy his curiosity, expand his horizons, relieve his tensions, assist him to understand himself and his fellows, and, above all, make him aware of and help him to live again the experience of the human race. No broad, general culture is possible without the ability to read and write.

Reading must never be considered as an isolated academic activity. It must always be related not only to all of the language arts but to the school curriculum as a whole. Very early in his school life and repeatedly through the grades a child should be made to understand that although reading may be difficult for him it is important and rewarding enough to require his best efforts. It is his right to know this; otherwise any joy in achievement will be thin. While the teacher at all times should encourage, praise where praise is not due is intellectual dishonesty. It cheats the child of a feeling of gradual mastery and a sense of developing power.

The intelligent *use* of reading should be every teacher's ultimate aim in reading instruction. So far no single method for that instruction can claim to be the most efficient for all. A teacher, however, must give careful consideration to the factors that may affect reading. She must make herself familiar with her pupils' individual differences and make adequate provision for those differences in her programme. She must have specific plans for making the programme interesting and she must have specific objectives for each child in her class. Perhaps it is not too obvious to add that she must know well the available books needed for instruction and for the children's extra reading, and provide in the classroom a wide range of supplementary materials at levels both above and below her grade. Above all, she must vary her teaching techniques, never losing sight of the fact that she is laying the foundations of reading skills which will result in permanent attitudes and growth. The teacher's appreciation and enjoyment of literature should create a healthy reading climate in the classroom.

A child will feel the urge to speak and write if he knows that his teacher has a sincere interest in what he has to express. Certainly he should be made aware of his errors; otherwise, he will adopt the attitude that English is too easy and not worth the expense of much effort or originality. The experienced teacher is one who has learned that the proper balance between praise and criticism is an interested and helpful approach to the child's problems in speech or writing.

Experiment would seem to support the argument that it is valuable to postpone reading until a child is ready for it. Reading-readiness is a fundamental problem, by no means restricted to the lower levels of instruction. Accordingly the programme in the Kindergarten is designed to build up a child's speaking vocabulary, instil habits of listening and of living with others, and provide experience with picture-books. He is then given an intelligence test, a readiness test, and a test on his interests. Do these tests adequately measure and identify those factors required for learning to read? Buttressed by the teacher's own judgment, the results of this battery of tests determine as well as can be done at present the readiness of the child to begin the process of formal reading. In this field there is a great need for research in testing more deeply, not only a child's preparedness for reading, but also his later stages in the reading process.

Because of any of a number of factors such as age, maturity, eye development, and lack of experience, it is possible that a child will not be expected to read even in Grade 1. There he will be given further reading-readiness experiences and tests to determine when it is time for him to join the reading group. Once in his appropriate reading group, a child, guided by his teacher, embarks on the several techniques for recognizing, analysing, and building words. The teacher must be at home with these techniques if progress is to be expected. If she has not been taught the skills at her Teachers' College, she must learn them, and learn them thoroughly. There may be other techniques worthy of investigation. How are teachers to be made aware of them, and, if new approaches are tried, what re-training of teachers will be required? Technical skills of this kind are important, since they lay the foundation for comprehension of what is read, for accurate spelling, for vocabulary building, and for writing, not only for the elementary grades but for all future education. Skills alone do not make reading attractive. Would it be a good idea at this point to ask to have a demonstration school where teachers might see different materials and methods and teaching techniques in action, using children of differing intelligence groups?

The teacher should have a pleasant voice, and should acquit herself well in the art of oral reading. She should use it to introduce her class to the best in children's stories. Such a teacher cannot help inspiring in children the desire to read for themselves. In their classroom there should be a browsing table on which lie attractive picture-books with large illustration and some print. In addition there should be an abundance of books that they may take home.

Each child in a reading group will have a reader or readers selected as being suited to the abilities of the group. For a skilful teacher in a well-equipped classroom all such readers are gateways to books of greater interest and value. But not all teachers have stores of additional books or skill in using them profitably. The readers issued by different publishers vary in content and vocabulary. Many of the texts most frequently used raise questions that call for careful study. Are some of these texts too low in vocabulary count, too dully repetitive, too vacuous? Many parents and teachers are asking if literary appreciation is being too long postponed. Are the units of work expected of the child too readily accomplished, his goals too conveniently close? Such questions are by no means limited to Grade 1, but are being asked at least up to Grade 6. Are style and content being forced to give way to attractive format and colourful illustration? Do the illustrations always correspond to the normal use of the word? Are some of them distracting enough to become traps for children seeking contextual clues? To what extent would further simplification in the illustration make it of value within itself and of use in the text? Would colour photographs be effective? Do the illustrations and the stories combine to make a book which is convincing to the children reading it? Are the stories told in living language? To what extent are the scrubbed, tidy, mannerly little suburbanites in their immaculate clothes, forever having fun, the happy inhabitants of a never-never land? How true to life is the expensively tailored and groomed mother, smilingly hanging out her wash? And with what mixed emotions do the children of less privileged families read, "Old cars are not good for much"? This comment occurs in one reader.

The reading texts, especially those used in Grade 1, are presumably the fruit of much highly skilled thought and labour and considerable painstaking scientific research. But is some of this research dated? Equally careful research has estimated the speaking vocabulary of a $6\frac{1}{2}$-year-old child to be anywhere from 2,500 to over 7,000 words. Even if we take the lower figure as valid, to set against it the total reading vocabulary expected of a child *at the end of* Grade 1 is to experience a shock. To put it another way, the reading vocabulary required of a child at the conclusion of Grade 1 is less than half of the speaking vocabulary of a child of 3.8 years of age, estimated at 700 words. This is a situation which invites queries. Should the texts contain fewer pointless repetitions? Should the stories move faster, be more believable and less antiseptic? Is there a job to be done here by interdisciplinary committees composed of psychologists, teachers, linguists, children's authors, and designers? What can be done about the classroom chaos traceable to the practice of bringing out "new" editions with minor changes, while previous editions are in the hands of some of the members of the class? Finally, more challenging material would be an improvement, something from our great literary heritage, commencing with nursery rhymes, fables, and folk-tales.

Writing, or at least the preparation for writing, can be dated from the time when a child first displays his motor skills in dabbling with paint and working with clay. In the home he sees letters arriving from Auntie, who lives far away but is able to "speak" to her relatives by means of a scrawl on a piece of paper. The need and the desire for written communication come early to the child. At first he dictates a message in an answer to Auntie. Then in the first year at school he may dictate a short letter through his teacher to a sick classmate. When he tells the teacher a story about a picture, she writes it down for him. Writing must surely appeal to him as a highly convenient skill, and it is not long before he learns to write his own name on personal belongings and at the bottom of his drawings. As he travels through the grades, the need for writing becomes increasingly obvious to him, but his early attempts are necessarily interrupted by his requests for help from the teacher. His first excursions will likely be story reproductions, narrative-descriptive pieces, imaginative stories, and letters.

In the intermediate division (Grades 4, 5, and 6) of the elementary school the reading skills become more refined. A child must learn when he ought to read slowly and when rapidly, and be able to see the inter-relation between main divisions and subordinate details. Now he must begin to outline mentally and make summaries, use a table of contents and an index, and learn the use of the dictionary and reference books, sources which require slow, careful reading. It is in this division of the elementary school that he will formulate the reading habits which will last a lifetime.

His reading texts in this division still display an undue preoccupation with word-count. Until he gets to Grade 6 he will find little in them of English literature to appeal to his imagination or to awaken his admiration. Even in Grade 6 the pickings will be thin enough. His teacher-pilot will be wise to steer his outside reading into those fascinating deeper channels that will make him realize the shallows of his schoolday readers.

By now his writing should begin to give him a growing sense of power. He will have many opportunities and some genuine demands for this skill. These are the years of the Cubs, the Brownies; minutes and reports need to be written. Perhaps, too, there is a school paper or magazine. He should write something every day, and ideally everything he writes should be at least seen by his teacher. Her attitude towards this work may make him or break him as a writer, for if her approach is other than friendly, the child will never express his real thoughts either orally or on paper. His goals should be ease, clarity, suitability, and originality. He should have much practice in the explanatory or expository type of writing as well as the descriptive and imaginative. This area of his elementary education is a most decisive one in shaping his skills in handwriting, spelling, usage, and sentence-sense.

In the senior section (Grades 7 and 8) a child should be guided in refining his reading skills, maturing his reading interests, and forming critical judgments. He should also learn to evaluate his own reading habits. As an assistance it would be well for him to keep a cumulative reading card on which he will list at least the titles of books he has read outside school. This will be of great value to his teacher as well as to himself.

By now he will have new interests in reading. It is hoped that he will be impressed by the emotional power of words and the telling effect of their use, and that both prose and poetry will appeal to him in their ability to endow ideas with strength and with beauty.

In his writing, his use of words should be expected to reveal an increasing discipline. He should write something every day, and perhaps let a class-mate check it critically before he makes a final copy for the teacher to read. Having recognized in his reading the quality of the writing of others, he should begin to take pride in his own. It is now not too early to learn the virtue of compressing and condensing, for good writers have discovered that they can double the impact of what they have written by cutting the number of words in half. His goals should be, as before, clarity, ease, suitability, and originality.

It is obvious that such a programme places a heavy responsibility on the teachers, the keystone of the educational arch. No one nowadays denies the national importance of education. Society should exercise care to see that only skilled and devoted hands are entrusted with the guidance of children in these early years. Children require encouragement, under-standing, and firmness. The public should remember that a task which is demanding enough in a classroom containing twenty-five or thirty boys and girls cannot successfully be performed with forty or more.

All elementary school teachers are teachers of English. An interested teacher creates interest in her students. A child's appreciation of English as a medium of great beauty and power may well depend on his teacher's use of the mother tongue, and on her attitude to it. She should appraise her own speech habits, her own ability to express herself in writing, and her own understanding and love of books. One of the encouraging features of our period in history is its faith in the ability to learn at any age.

Teachers worthy of the profession learn constantly. To speak, read, and write well are admirable goals for teachers as well as children.

Some teachers of reading received their training at a time when the phonetic techniques were out of fashion. A thorough knowledge of systematic word techniques is indispensable for satisfactory teaching of reading. Those who lack such knowledge should proceed to fill the gap in their equipment. For all teachers fresh and varied approaches give vitality to the classroom, keep them alert, and contribute to the concept of education as a process of growth and discovery.

3. LITERATURE

Although there is no definition of literature that is universally acceptable, there are areas of fairly general agreement about its nature and function in society. It shows so complete a fusion of language with thought that one has become part of the texture of the other. It provides continuity and tradition in a culture. It brings delight to untold millions. It gives permanent form to what might otherwise be only passing moments of insight into the nature of man and human life. It stimulates the imagination and provides material for fruitful reflection. It takes the reader beyond himself and makes him aware of the infinite variety as well as the common heritage of humanity. Perhaps we might venture to describe literature as the arrangement of language in significant and appropriate patterns, providing through imagination and reflection an additional dimension to the actual experience of living.

It has frequently been suggested that, since the full appreciation of literature demands maturity, it is foolish to attempt to teach it to the young. This seems to us of the same order of logic as forbidding a boy who may later become an engineer to play with a meccano set. Of course a child cannot fully appreciate literature, but literature is, or should be, one of the most important influences in his gradual maturing. Our problem is to find the best ways through which the child (and the man) can be brought into vital contact with literature at various stages of his development.

For the more fortunate this contact will have preceded school attendance. A child who has not from infancy become gradually familiar with the world of nursery rhymes, folk-tales, simple poems, myth and legend, fairy-tales, and Bible stories has missed a great deal. The evidence is clear that reading to a child increases his eagerness to learn to read for himself and that a boy or girl so read to has already begun to form the rudiments of literary taste. The telling and reading of stories and poems, together with the attempt to answer the child's questions in a way which is both true and simple, and the carrying on of intelligent conversation with him, are fundamental obligations of good parents and teachers.

There is wide, and sometimes bitter, divergence of opinion about the literary quality of material used in teaching children to read. The argument for simplicity of presentation seems to have a strong logical basis. Similarly the idea of a controlled vocabulary seems to be common sense. Yet the simplicity is often deceptive; what appears simple may, on closer examination, not only prove more complex than was thought at first, but may also contain illogical quirks of the language which can be both baffling and misleading for the child. The sort of control exercised over vocabulary often has a highly doubtful psychological and linguistic basis. This whole problem, including the connection between speech and reading, and the effect of the shift from the relatively sophisticated level both of language and of concept in speech to the sort of material found in basic readers, needs even more study (or perhaps study from a different point of view) than it has been given. A fairly large body of experimental evidence has been built up which suggests that material of some literary merit could be introduced at an earlier stage.

What sort of literature, then, should be included in early readers? This is part of the question raised by Jerome Bruner in *The Process of Education*. Are there in every subject basic principles of structure which can be taught in some form to every person at every age? The application of this theory to literature is still far from clear, but one starting point might be the story. Even a very young child understands instinctively Aristotle's idea of the story as "the imitation of an action." He is quite aware of the practice, if not the theory, of plot structure; conflict, complication, suspense, climax, *dénouement* are realities to him, even though the words are far beyond his controlled vocabulary. He is also aware of character and the interplay of character and action. He is acutely aware of some aspects at least of atmosphere—indeed more sensitive in this respect than most adults. It seems too bad to confine his own reading any longer than necessary to the rather soggy unadventures of Dick, Jane, and Baby Sally.

Simple poems with merit in thought, sound, and diction make suitable fare at an early stage. A child's sense of rhythm is instinctive—perhaps deeper-rooted than we know. He has a quick ear for sound and readily appreciates effects like rhyme and imitative harmony. It may be significant that the first selections "read" by a child (long before he goes to school) are likely to be the jingles of the television "commercials." Perhaps these techniques could be employed to worthier ends. The same narrative or descriptive impression in prose and in verse can become the basis for comparative judgments which are often remarkably shrewd and will be invaluable in later definition of various sorts of literature.

There seems, too, to be a good deal of literary potential in the new discoveries of science and associated fields: a world of romance and adventure not altogether unlike earlier tales of conquest, chivalry, war, and exploration.

The success of the policy of increasing literary dividends in the early reading programme will depend to an even greater extent than at later stages on the teachers, because at this point even the brightest child cannot so readily go beyond and above his instructor as he will be able to do later. A teacher who herself lacks literary taste and sensitivity will find it hard to strike the divine spark from her students. But even the poorest teacher should do better with the best materials. The children can hardly fail to benefit. And perhaps in the effort to communicate to her students something of the essence of literature, this teacher may herself discover the significance of this thing which has hitherto eluded her.

Once a child has learned to read well enough to be able to read by himself and to want to do so, he has obviously passed an extraordinarily important milestone on his educational journey. This takes us back to the problem of the best ways to bring him into vital contact with literature at various stages of development. We are tempted to say simply, "Once he has learned to read, let him read as much as possible." But such a statement, although it contains a great deal of the truth, is not adequate.

Perhaps it is relevant at this point to mention briefly the conclusions of Piaget and the psychologists of the Geneva school. They speak of the development of a child's way of looking at things as consisting of three stages. The first is the "pre-operational" period, in which his mental work consists mainly in establishing relationships between experience and action, that is, in attempting to manipulate the world around him through action and speech. (One is tempted to observe that many people apparently never pass beyond this stage.) The second stage is the period of "concrete operations"—an operation being defined as a means of getting data about the real world into the mind and there transforming them so that they can be organized and used selectively in the solution of problems. Such operations are confined largely to immediate problems or problems within the range of the child's experience, that is, to concrete and practical situations rather than to abstract and theoretical propositions. Then, somewhere between the ages of ten and fourteen years, the child passes into the stage of "formal operations," where he begins to develop the kind of logical thought-patterns characteristic of the mathematician, the scientist, and the philosopher. These developments, they suggest, can be either speeded up or slowed down by the way he is taught in school. (There are, of course, many other influences, but this is the one with which we are mainly concerned.) The theory seems well worth further study and experiment to see how both materials and methods of teaching might be improved.

Alfred North Whitehead has a different, though not contradictory, theory of development. He speaks of a child as passing from an "age of romance," through an "age of precision," to an "age of generalization." Again this theory needs to be examined and tested to see what implications it holds for the school system.

The grades from 2 to 6 would seem to combine the "age of romance" with the stage of "concrete operations." Since Chesterton says that the great truths about human life are all contained in paradoxes, we should not be discouraged by this one. What it means, in terms of literature, is that the curriculum, if it is to suit the child at this stage, must contain a range of material from fantasy to stories and poems very close to his own experience. The readers designed for these grades show fairly clearly an attempt at something of this sort. We feel that there is still plenty of room for improvement, particularly in the selections of poetry, which are on occasion inferior to verse some of the youngsters themselves write, but there is literary nourishment here for a teacher to use in building a healthy appreciation among her students. There is, of course, no reason why the material for lessons in literature should always come from the readers. Lists of suitable selections prepared by really good teachers, perhaps including some suggestions for the handling of the material, might well be made available.

Much of the child's literary development will come from his own reading. At this stage, children are likely to divide themselves fairly permanently into readers and non-readers. What can be done to encourage a youngster to read and to lead him to prefer the best in literature?

Perhaps the most important factor here is the availability of books. The child who is brought up in a home which is filled with interesting and attractive books and journals representing a broad range of taste will have a hard time to avoid becoming a reader. Unfortunately, there are far too few such homes. Besides, it should be natural for him to associate books with school. It is rather a curious phenomenon that, although almost no one would deny the central role of a library in university education, so little attention has been paid until recently to library facilities in elementary and secondary schools. One of the most important policies established by the Toronto Board of Education in recent years is a plan which will eventually bring library service, both for recreational reading and for research in connection with studies, to every elementary as well as every secondary school. It is hard to exaggerate the significance of this development. Although the new collections are comparatively small, they are excellent in quality and will no doubt be rapidly supplemented, particularly in the area of recreational reading. The service will also be extended as quickly as possible to cover all the schools. Much of the success of the plan will depend on the teachers who act as librarians and on the co-operation of principals in arranging for students to get the maximum benefit from library facilities.

Research and experiment seem to be needed to find ways of integrating more closely the study of literature with language study and writing. One idea about the way in which such research might be carried out is contained in the suggestions of the Modern Language Association's pamphlet *An Articulated English Program.* A simplified form of their projected organization would be the selection of a limited number of schools and teachers in one locality, such as Toronto, to be gathered along with some university people into seminar groups which could design experimental programmes, gather evidence from their actual use with classes, assess the results, and modify the programmes accordingly. Such research and experiment should be regarded as a continuing process rather than a quick method of producing the perfect curriculum in English. A similar method might be used to discover ways of achieving better correlation between English and other subjects of study. The question of whether a person can think beyond the range of his vocabulary may be debatable, but the importance of language in every field of knowledge can hardly be questioned.

Moving now from the junior to the intermediate grades, what changes in approach or shifts of emphasis are appropriate? This move seems to correspond roughly to the advance from Whitehead's "age of romance" to the "age of precision" and from the stage of "concrete operations" to that of "formal operations." This does not mean that the study of literature, having hitherto been fun, now becomes work. If such study is to accomplish its purpose, it must at all stages combine the joy of freedom in play with the satisfaction inherent in achievement through disciplined effort.

The extension of his own experience through literature gives a child both pleasure and increased knowledge. It shows him new patterns of behaviour and broadens the base for his standards of judgment. It can stimulate or relax him, set his curiosity and imagination racing along new and exciting paths or let him simply sit and absorb with delight the sights and sounds portrayed by the writer. It is, if the opportunity is provided, the most important influence in his intellectual development; it gives him a chance to stop and think about what he has read, to see problems and work out solutions, to observe relationships which he had never before suspected, to contemplate as himself and yet out of himself, because he is freed from the compelling pressures of his immediate environment.

By this time a child (is it too early to begin calling him a student?) should have read widely enough to be aware of the different forms and the recurrent themes which are, perhaps, the basic principles of structure in literature. It seems, then, like a logical time for him to be taught something more about these forms and the ways in which form and content are related. He has already been introduced to the technique of discussion in literary study, not the clash of opposing emotional reactions, but the combining and sifting of different impressions and interpretations leading toward fuller understanding and appreciation. From this point on, such discussion should become increasingly valuable because the student has more knowledge and better judgment to bring to the task. But we must tread warily here. It is easy to let literature become merely a springboard for launching into amateur psychiatry and sociology, and there is nothing more terrifying than the frequently smug group of little people glibly nattering about some matter which is far beyond the range of their experience and comprehension, in the mistaken belief that they are becoming "mature" and "life-adjusted." The study of longer books— novels, poems, plays—makes it easier to draw the attention of a student to the way the writer has organized and shaped his material to create the effect he had in mind. Comparison of different literary forms and the ways in which these differences affect the material presented is within the grasp of students at this stage. Discussion of similar themes treated from different points of view and with different techniques gives students some insight into the theory of literature.

Already the problem of differing tastes and abilities has made itself felt in various ways. Some students are bright; others are dull. Some have a flair for literature; others seem bored. Should there really be any attempt to have them all take the same course? These differences among individuals have received a good deal of attention in the last thirty years and, even before that, any teacher with common sense was quite aware of them. The way the problem is handled is an indication of a fundamental philosophy of education. It seems reasonable that the children at the extremes of the range of ability need very special treatment which may, perhaps, entail separating them from the others. But is it desirable to subdivide the rest? (We are speaking of English; the same reasoning may not apply to other subjects.) Is not what these young people have in common as human beings more important and more relevant than their differences? Moreover, does not the very nature of literature provide for and suggest the advantage of study on a very broad front? We have all known youngsters who were not brilliant students, but who showed surprising maturity and sensitivity in the study of literature. Conversely it is not uncommon to find a child whose grasp of mathematics, for example, suggests near genius, but who is singularly obtuse in his literary reactions. We are obviously dealing here with something more than just intelligence, and, although intellect is involved (and it is well to remember that intellect and intelligence are by no means the same thing), it is more, too, than a matter of intellect. Perhaps it is the very essence of humanity that we are attempting to cultivate through the study of literature.

During this stage of development it is quite common to find students less enthusiastic than they have previously been about reading and the study of literature. This phenomenon has not escaped public notice and the blame for it, as well as for many other undesirable situations, has frequently been laid at the door of the teacher. It is an easy explanation and may well be true. There are plenty of poor teachers, although this does not make teaching unique among the professions. And the very good teacher who succeeds in conquering all the difficulties seems to prove the point. But the difficulties are there and, once more, there seems to be a profitable field for research and experiment. What are the best ways to impart to the study of literature a sense of importance and urgency that will overcome the natural reluctance to accept the increasing load of disciplined thinking, which is hard work? What can parents do to encourage their children to read and discuss? What effects have the development of other interests at this stage, the change from elementary to secondary school, the multiplicity of teachers, the growing conflict between imposed discipline and the desire for independence? The answers to such questions are urgent if education is going to be able to fulfil even a part of the expectations which are being increasingly associated with formal schooling. And, although many of these expectations seem quite unreasonable, to what other agency in society can we turn for relief?

By the time a student reaches Grades 11 and 12 he has, presumably, also reached the stage of "formal operations" or the "age of generalization." If he has shown reasonable aptitude in his study of language, has made a classroom acquaintance with different forms of literature, and has read widely on his own, he should be prepared for a fairly demanding and challenging critical study of literary works of some complexity. The "if" raises once more the question whether all students should be given the same course in English literature—the same books, the same method, the same pace. The case for "streaming" is not really clear, in spite of its wide practice. M. M. Lewis in *The Importance of Illiteracy* (London: Harrap, 1953) has pointed out that a distinction between "academic" and "non-academic" types of students has never really been established, although most school organization in Europe rests on that basic assumption. Clearly, research and experiment are again needed. Meantime, common sense will continue to keep the good teacher from going too far off the track.

Courses at this stage tend generally to break down into bits and pieces; students frequently get the impression that they are studying a series of individual books and poems rather than studying English literature. Is this a point where some of the basic themes of literature might be used as a framework within which a student could observe them as treated by different writers, in different literary genres, at different periods of history with their differing social milieux? Might there not be experiment with methods of teaching: large group instruction, individual reading and research in improved libraries, correlation with composition through the writing of essays on relevant topics, and the reading and discussion of these essays in groups smaller than the normal class? Not only are experiments along new lines needed, but it must be remembered that the success of any method may depend as much on the teacher, class, and school as on the scheme itself.

Although we believe that the study of literature should be a continuing process, we feel that this study at the Grade 13 and university levels should be dealt with separately in this report. The consideration, in both cases, will include the whole field of English, and, in the case of Grade 13, will deal more specifically with courses and examinations than has been done at other levels.

In all of our discussions, and throughout this report, we kept coming back to the teacher as the focal point in any plan to improve the teaching of English. A teacher of literature enjoys a unique relationship with his students. Together they are exploring and discussing the words of men and women who, gifted with imagination, insight, and the power of language, have left these records of their impressions of man and human life.

What qualities of mind and heart must a teacher have to make that relationship most helpful to his students?

First of all he must know what he is attempting to teach. Far too many teachers of English throughout Ontario are so only because making them teachers of English seemed essential to the proper functioning of the school timetable. Critic-teachers agree almost unanimously that the chief fault among student-teachers of English from the Ontario College of Education is that they simply do not know enough about the subject. No course in methodology can overcome this defect.

Then, he must have respect for his students—for their potentialities, if not for their achievements. The teacher who despises his students should not be allowed to teach literature. He should have a taste for scholarship and always remain a student as well as a teacher. (This is a matter of great importance, and of almost insuperable difficulty with the sort of working conditions most teachers have.) He should be able to understand the world of his students without himself being of that world, should be a friend but not a chum. He should be a man of taste and discrimination, not just in literature, but in all aspects of living. He should be a man of broad interests, who is aware of the importance of other fields of knowledge and the way in which all fit into the general structure. He should be engaged in the pursuit of wisdom rather than knowledge, but should make his students aware that all knowledge can aid in that pursuit.

4. COMPOSITION

Everyone would agree that to enable young people to write as well as possible is one of the chief functions of the English teacher. Yet no subject is more clouded with controversy and confusion than that of teaching writing. What should be taught, at what stages, and in what ways are questions constantly debated. A multiplicity of aims, activities, and advice leaves all but the most independent teachers bewildered.

Though it is assumed that education should produce good writers, the term "good" is seldom defined or analysed. Good writing is no simple process to be perfected by a neat formula. Study of the backgrounds of outstanding writers reveals no consistent pattern of preparation. Many have had a limited amount of formal schooling. All writing, however, contains the ingredients of an art: selection of material, a shaping form, and appropriate expression. As a young writer sets down his responses to experience and knowledge, he must be aware of all these ingredients. Yet there is no generally accepted standard by which his work can be judged, nor are the judges themselves always capable of writing well. Some teachers consider that interesting content and freshness in observation compensate for lapses in grammatical relationships. Others value a "correct" but pedestrian treatment of a subject. Still others look for a combination of significant content and conscious graces of style. For a few, spontaneity is all-important. Uncertainty about what should be expected of young writers at various stages, and the problem of maintaining a delicate balance of judgment between what is said and the way in which it is said, are factors adding to the difficulty of teaching composition.

Most people would agree that a high-school graduate should be expected to write competent prose with something to say, thought clearly developed, and expression free from serious errors. Most of the criticism directed at the schools suggests that their failure here is conspicuous. Though it is difficult to secure evidence of declining standards, there seems to be a general impression that the disciplines governing thought and usage have slackened. Whether through carelessness or ignorance, young people who should know better are casual about the basic good manners of language observances. But lapses from standard usage are not the only defects of writing today. Much of the writing of adults is diffuse and pretentious, vague in meaning and graceless in style. Business men, social scientists, candidates for doctoral degrees, people engaged in many branches of education produce bloated prose, without being disturbed by the fog of obscurity. This disease, which has been labelled "gobbledygook," "gargantuan," and "barnacular" by those who have diagnosed it, is seldom found in young writers. Like gout, it comes with advancing years, and, like gout, it frustrates movement. There is cause for public concern about writing, but it must be concern for writing at all stages. To be effective it must be followed by consideration of purposes and problems, by analysis, and by constructive suggestion and action.

Much of the confusion about teaching composition has arisen from failure to understand that there are different kinds of writing, demanding different treatment. The motives that prompt a writer are varied: a wish or need to record or convey information, or the results of accumulated knowledge; an urge to capture some aspect of experience; a desire to release a compelling idea or emotion; a consciousness that some fragment or combination of life's many facets may be given artistic shape. The motive is often utilitarian, in business, for instance, and in much of the compiling, recording, and interpreting of information required in the process of education. Sometimes writing is in the nature of discovery, the writer finding himself as he puts into words his responses to life. For a few, writing is a form of possession, the writer driven as much as driving, loving his art and yet pursued by it, excited by the creative impulse, yet requiring of himself the most strenuous kind of discipline.

Whatever the motive, certain ingredients are common to all kinds of writing: an idea or impulse, a selection of material, form or shape, a choice and arrangement of words. In all kinds of writing the ingredients can be fused only after much practice. Competence and good craftsmanship can be developed by most writers in some kinds of writing; artistry in one or more forms can be expected from a few. It does not follow that because excellence in some forms is rare, they should not be attempted. Through the search for words and pattern a writer may learn much about precision and design. A distinguished scientist once recommended to his students the writing of poetry as a way of discovering the need for precision in the use of words. Judgment will be required of a teacher in order to maintain proportion and emphasis in the selection of forms for practice, but an occasional daring experiment may sharpen perception and add new dimensions to experience.

Certain types of writing that are essential to the process of education *must* be practised in the schools until students are proficient in them. Their principles and techniques should be taught in the English classroom, but their practice must be carried into other classrooms and supervised by other teachers. Every teacher of science, history, and geography is, whether he realizes it or not, a teacher of the expository forms of language. Without his interest and concern, student writing in his field will be inadequate, and the students' education the poorer. One of the most urgent needs in education is the coming together of teachers of English and those in other fields requiring the use of written English, to discover how the teaching and learning may be reinforced. The separate disciplines are apt to forget that education, in Whitehead's phrase, is a seamless garment.

Damage is sometimes done to the cause of teaching writing by the over-use of slogans or catchwords. Such a term is "creative writing." There is need for an imaginative approach to children's writing, and much has been done in recent years to stimulate such an approach. At no other period has there been such success in capturing the directness and freshness of children's response to experience. But the term "creative writing," applied to writing in the schools, has no precise meaning, and is often misinterpreted. Sometimes it indicates merely a revulsion against the stereotyped set piece; occasionally it is interpreted as the unrestricted flow of words on to paper. The hard work, and the long period of shaping before the final form is achieved, are ingredients not contemplated by all who advocate "creative writing." A teacher of limited imagination, antagonized by the shapelessness that he thinks is implied by the term, may be driven into a more and more "practical" approach. Two, says C. P. Snow, is an awkward number, suggesting an *either–or* instead of *both–and.* It should be possible to encourage different kinds of writing. To keep alive the sense of wonder, to encourage the keen observation that sees the world afresh, and to find significance and pattern in commonplace or fantastic experiences are admirable aims that are being reflected in present-day text-books. So, too, is the development of thought through training in the accumulation of evidence, the setting of facts in order, and the drawing of conclusions. To maintain this balance in writing is a major problem for teachers of English.

Within recent years more serious consideration has been given to the teaching of writing than at any previous time. In recent books and articles by teachers of experience and judgment there is surprising agreement on certain basic issues. The views of the Secondary Masters in England and of contributors to the quarterly, *The Use of English,* are echoed by many of the writers in the American teachers' magazine, *The English Journal.* It is agreed that students should spend more time in practising writing than in listening to a teacher's advice on how to write. Good writers are the best teachers, and exposure to them is infectious. It is no accident that the students who write best are usually those who read widely. Every teacher of composition should be able to introduce his classes to the best writing, much of it contemporary, beyond the selections given in text-books. Effective writing has a pattern. Perceiving the pattern is part of the writer's task, as the word *composition* implies. Most schoolboys and girls are convinced that "inspiration" results in a spontaneous outpouring that needs no revision. They find it difficult to believe that authors plan, reflect, revise, rewrite. They must be led to see that idea, form, and expression require craftsmanship if a writer's purpose is to be realized. Here the study of literature and that of writing are complementary. Through reading and discussion young writers should discover the requirements of different types of writing. Obviously, once purpose and pattern have been perceived, a writer still has problems of expression. There is general agreement that exercises requiring the correction of faulty sentences, or the memorizing of errors to be avoided are of little value as a prelude to writing. Language study and grammar are necessary, but not in this negative form.

The assumptions are that, given the stimulus of interesting or challenging subjects, the prospect of a sympathetic reader, and enough practice to make writing a habit, most young people can learn to express themselves directly and coherently in writing. All experienced teachers agree that the teaching and assessing of writing requires knowledge and appreciation of this art, and of children and their development. There is a consensus of opinion that teachers submerged by the weight of student writing to be read cannot retain the freshness and vision required for this work.

Consideration of the ideas presented above raises questions of emphasis and procedure in teaching. How is a sense of form to be encouraged? How does a learner adapt the disciplines involved in the study of the sentence to his purposes, and discover the flexibility that lies within those disciplines? How can writers who show special promise be encouraged? How are persistent violations of the relationships of normative grammar to be dealt with, and how can an understanding of those relationships be strengthened through writing?

The answers may lie in an increased awareness for both teachers and pupils of the unity of English studies. The relationships between reading and writing, grammar or language study and writing should be strengthened. In earlier times the study of rhetoric established ties between other men's speech or writing and that of the student. In modern education the study of English has become more and more a number of separate activities. To re-establish a synthesis would require careful planning, not necessarily sweeping changes in content, but rearrangement for the purposes of emphasis and coherence. The room in which writing is practised or discussed should be one in which books are displayed. Discussions of reading, the examination of models, and from time to time the imitation of their forms are ways of strengthening the relationship between reading and writing. The study of sentences, their structure and relationships, should accompany the practice of writing, with an emphasis on the use of patterns and relationships to clarify meaning and add strength and grace to expression. Identification of errors should come from the young writer's own work, not from text-book samples. To be fully effective, grammar must be seen as a basis for the art of rhetoric. There is great need for study, demonstration, and experiment in order to discover ways of making the relationship between language study and writing more rewarding.

An important ingredient in learning to write is discussion and revision. A writer at any stage finds it difficult to read his own work with detachment. Many outstanding writers have been helped by the comments of a wise friend, an editor, a questioning tutor, or a book. The work of a young writer in the school or in the university will be heard or read, sometimes by his fellows, usually by his teacher. So far no effective substitute has been found for the careful assessment of student writing, for constructive suggestion, for improvement, and for revision. Students are notoriously reluctant to proofread their own work carefully. Many of the blunders so much deplored by critics of the schools, and so irritating to teachers, are the result of carelessness. The practice of re-reading and revising before work is handed in should be emphasized. Teachers have been too ready to accept slipshod manuscripts. On their part, teachers should read with some other purposes than the pursuit of errors. The extent to which a writer has achieved his purpose, any especially effective passages, suggestions for improvement, references for reading on matters of structure and usage—these should be noted either during an interview or by written comment. The assessing of writing is not easy; the securing of a university degree does not confer the ability to do it well. Again there is need for assistance to young teachers. Even within the university young teachers should mark their first papers with the assistance of senior staff members.

Such treatment of written work places a heavy burden on teachers of English, a burden which, until recently, administrators were reluctant to acknowledge. Within the past year there have been welcome signs of change. The number of promising teachers of English who have requested to be transferred to other subjects has been alarming. The reason given, the burden of marking which the conscientious teacher could neither neglect nor handle adequately, has made imperative some action. Publication of the J. B. Conant report, *The American High School Today* (New York: McGraw-Hill, 1959), has pointed a direction. Dr. Conant's recommendations for the spending of increased time on composition, and his suggestion of a ratio not exceeding one hundred students to one teacher of composition, indicate the importance that is being placed in the United States on the student's efforts to gain control of the written language. Similar recognition for Canadian schools, and experiments with the use of lay readers, may help to attract teachers with knowledge and talent, and will offer relief to those who have been overburdened.

What further can be done to improve the teaching of writing? It is important that teachers be kept informed of investigations dealing with the nature and learning of language. Contributions are being made from many sources: from the linguists, from the students of aesthetics, and from the mathematical logicians. As the Bruner report indicates, discoveries about learning in the sciences and in mathematics may have application to the field of language. Interest in the way in which the child learns and uses language has already proved illuminating and may provide the basis for a broadly sequential programme.

Here Whitehead's differentiation of the three stages in the development of a child may again be referred to. The stage of romance, prompted by wonder, and leading to exciting discoveries about the world and its creatures, he gave as lasting from the age of eight or thereabouts to eleven or twelve. When the excitement of first discovery is followed by the desire to *know* more exactly, there comes the age of precision, from eleven or twelve to fifteen. This in turn is succeeded by the age of generalization. Whether Whitehead's premises are fully acceptable or not, they have bearing on the teaching of writing in their suggestion of release for the early years of schooling, followed by increasing control, and by training in the methods of developing thought. The child's first stage of romance and of wonder is the period of discovery of himself and of the world about him. The expression of such experience in writing is a way of focussing attention on it. If observation is keen, if responses to sights, sounds, and situations are captured, writing with individuality and freshness can be produced. C. S. Lewis, a writer of distinction himself, comments on the clear, sharp observation and the precision of sense impressions in such writing.

As a child reads more, his writing may become more imitative, to the distress of the teacher who emphasizes originality. The imitation may be turned to good account, for the writer may become more aware of form, of the search for credibility and the apt word. The editors of a collection of children's writing point out that during this phase, the important development is the extension of the way in which a child looks at life. The tales of sensationalism and violence often characteristic of this period usually give way to a further stage of deepened understanding.

The stage of precision, after the age of eleven or twelve, requires an increasing awareness of form, closer attention to the organization of the whole, and to the structure and relationship of sentences. This is the stage at which the range of materials can profitably be extended to include other school subjects, the stage at which "creative writing," in the sense in which it is often used, is balanced by the accumulation of facts and of evidence, their arrangement in logical order, and the drawing of conclusions. Emphasis on thought and arrangement need not mean dullness. Much of the best writing of our day is informative, descriptive, precise in its choice of words, clear in style, but imaginative in its perception. Too often the imagination is invoked by a young writer to excuse vague, woolly writing. A sharpened awareness of the need for clear thought and order should be extended to the shaping of sentences and the observing of grammatical relationships. Errors of this kind now, as later, are usually caused by failure to complete a thought. If the thought is clear, the relationships are usually sound. If not, drill is necessary. Perhaps the disciplines of this age of precision have been somewhat neglected in our schools in the belief that spontaneity might be stifled. This is a subject for discussion and investigation.

With such training, boys and girls should be ready for the work of the senior grades. The study of more advanced examples of prose, and the use of these for experiments in writing in different styles can be a constructive, not merely an imitative, activity. There should be a growing awareness of the flexibility and the resources of language. Study of the devices for clarifying, illustrating, and developing thought should provide the tools for papers on subjects that encourage a writer to use and extend his knowledge, become more aware of current problems and issues, and more able to analyse and comment. The paper that requires the exploration of a subject, careful organization, and the use of supporting evidence is a step towards the desire for synthesis that Whitehead says is characteristic of this stage.

Many teachers, and many text-books, already follow some such developing programme, but the practice is by no means general. Teachers often fail to take the long view. Involved in a multitude of daily activities, they are not aware of the sequence of writing through the grades. The best books are not always known; the pamphlets giving advice on procedures may be too general or too detailed; the department head may think of giving help only with the grade in which the teacher works. The lecture in the teachers' college is not the solution. The issues and problems posed by student writing do not appear until the teacher has tried to teach and become aware of his difficulties.

Clamour for improved standards in writing is pointless without teachers who have an appreciation of writing and some skill in its practice. This is not always guaranteed by a pass-mark in Grade 13 or by a degree from a university. Indeed, until recently, it was possible to enter a teachers' college without Grade 13 standing in *both* English Literature and English Composition. One of these was sufficient. There must be many teachers in both elementary and secondary schools who shrink from the thought of teaching writing. Sometimes the chief equipment brought to the subject is an otherwise blank space on a timetable.

Even the teachers who have had university courses in English may find themselves hesitant about teaching composition. Most of the writing in the university has been in the form of critical analysis, not necessarily the best preparation for teaching writing. Perhaps this is a question worthy of some consideration.

There is urgent need for searching out ways of informing teachers about various kinds of writing, approaches to their problems, methods of collecting, arranging, and presenting material, and improving the grasp of standard usage. If opportunities could be offered, the number of teachers interested might prove to be surprising. Anyone who has listened to writers discussing their craft alone, in groups, or in print is aware of the excitement that can be stirred. The listener discovers that the professional's problems are his, with a difference of degree. Something of this excitement might be engendered by classes for teachers in lectures and small groups, by reading lists, by demonstrations, and by writing groups. Professional improvement classes of all kinds are offered, many of them narrow in content. Here is a problem that cries for attention from people who through their knowledge and nature are competent to offer guidance. Such courses might be used as credit for advanced standing. They should be attended and assessed by representative teachers at *all* levels—elementary school, secondary school, and the university. Critics at each stage who have censured what is done, or left undone, by others might discover common problems.

Along with discussion a series of experiments should be undertaken to investigate which writing procedures are effective at different stages. The ways in which grammar and language structure should be presented, the amount and nature of this type of study in various grades, the problem of relating grammar to writing and speech also require study. Demonstrations and lectures by able teachers would be of help to the many inexperienced newcomers flooding the classrooms. There are challenging prospects for the years ahead.

5. LANGUAGE STUDY

Literature depends upon a sense of form, a feeling for the art of selection, which creates a design or pattern from the infinite variety of human experience. It is, therefore, easy to forget that a student's earliest experience with form and pattern in his study of English is in language itself. In fact, long before a child ever comes to school, he has begun to grasp the sense of form and pattern which is necessary in using our complex communicative system, human language. Literature itself can only be understood against the design and pattern which is called language, for this provides the primary material out of which literature is made. Since the various areas of the study of English are quite naturally integrated because they deal with the English language, it is not surprising to discover that the treatment of language study is a central concern of the school programme.

Naturally, language study enters into every department of English studies. It is concerned in composition, in literary study, in first grade reading, and in literary analysis in the graduate school at university. The formal study of English which attempts to describe and analyse the English language is extremely important to the entire subject. No area of the English programme, however, is more likely to become involved in controversy, because, of all his properties, each man is most intimately connected with his modes of speech and expression. Certainly the questions of how much formal language study, what kind of formal language study, and at what levels, are critical points of controversy in present-day discussions of education.

The formal study of language in the school programme involves such diverse activities as the teaching of reading skills, the teaching of spelling, word-building, the teaching of meaning (semantics), the use of the dictionary (lexicography), the sounds of English (phonetics and phonology), and English grammar. Many of these activities are not recognized as part of the formal teaching of language and consequently much of the relationship between them can be lost. It is, however, apparent that all of these activities are closely related and are intrinsic parts of the formal language teaching. Consequently, the formal study of language can be expected to have an important influence on the teaching of writing, the teaching of the spoken language, the teaching of literature and literary criticism, and the improvement of reading. Since the last fifty years have seen considerable advance in linguistic theory, it should be possible to find more effective and more economical ways of handling many of these teaching problems. The application of linguistic knowledge to the teaching of spelling or word-building, to the improvement of the teaching of phonetics or semantics or lexicography, may well result in improvements in unexpected parts of the programme of English studies. Considerable further study of some of the possible applications of linguistic knowledge to teaching in these areas is needed. At the moment it is difficult to determine how extensive the improvements brought about might be.

The most debated and least understood part of the programme of formal language study has to do with the study of English grammar. First of all, there are those who confuse grammar with the teaching of rules for writing correctly. Others confuse it with the analysis of empty sentences that have never been used anywhere except in grammar books. Still others find it in the learning of tables of tenses, cases, and the like which have little or no reality in English as it actually is. Each of these points of view, however, is a mistake. First, they confuse two very different types of grammar: the descriptive, which tells how language is constructed, and the normative, which tells us how we ought to speak or write. Second, descriptive grammar need not be confined to the structure of the artificial or the contrived; it can be applied to the living language in speech and writing. Nor does normative grammar have to depend on a list of artificial rules, for it can and should emanate from the active usage of the society of educated speakers and writers. Recent controversy on the role of grammar in the schools and the university has brought dramatic attention to bear upon multiple confusions involved in discussions about grammar and has contributed greatly to the emphasis on a return to the formal study of grammar in both the descriptive and the normative sense.

A major contribution to the study of grammar has been made by the newer studies in structural and descriptive linguistics, which have had considerable influence in both England and the United States. The late J. R. Firth, professor of linguistics at the University of London and president of the Philological Society of Great Britain, summarized the linguist's view of the problem of grammar study in the schools when he observed: "The decline of grammar, as we have known it, especially of school grammar is probably due to its naivety and obvious incompleteness and inadequacy, both in formal description and in dealing with meaning. It has fallen down on the job." Firth's words have been echoed by many in the United Kingdom and in the United States, including professors from Harvard, Yale, Cornell, Chicago, Columbia, Michigan, California, and Texas. As a result a controversy between the linguists (so-called) and the traditional grammarians has developed. Both sides, however, emphasize the importance of formal study of grammar in the school programme. The more fair-minded advocates of both sides also point out that while grammar study is important, it should not be over-emphasized, nor should it be isolated from the teaching of composition or the study of literature.

The prestige and professional qualifications of the linguists make it apparent that their position is to a considerable degree a healthy corrective. Just how this could or should affect the teaching of grammar in the schools is a matter that deserves careful study. The linguists, for example, all assert the primacy of speech: by this they mean that speech is fundamental to any kind of language analysis. Therefore, they assert that there are certain fundamental and important distinctions between the written and the spoken language. If such positions are correct, some rearrangement of the formal programme of language study should certainly result. By asserting a difference between speech and writing and by asserting the primacy of speech, the linguists are not, however, suggesting that the written language is of less value than the spoken language. They are just emphasizing that a solid understanding of the dynamics of speech is a prior necessity to understanding the special refinements and effects of writing. A formal study of speech and writing, rather than the present tendency to emphasize writing and forget speech, would certainly enrich and improve the programme of language study.

Certain aspects of the distinction between the spoken and written languages are beyond debate and are of central importance to a student of composition. A knowledge of the prosodic system (pitch, stress, and juncture) in spoken English is of considerable assistance to him in understanding why certain kinds of structures are clear and suitable in speech, but lead to confusion and ambiguity in writing. Furthermore, a knowledge of these features of speech will have important influences on his study and appreciation of poetry, dramatic literature, and prose. The contemporary linguist's ability to describe the system of sounds of the language in considerable detail should be made available to the secondary school student to aid him in appreciating the miracle of speech in its relations to literature and in life.

Apart from their emphasis on the primacy of speech and the difference between speech and writing, contemporary linguists insist that their approach to the conventional aspect of grammar is more systematic and formal (in the proper sense of the study of form). Much controversy has been carried on over the traditional definitions and the definitions of the newer grammarians, but little understanding has resulted. No fully successful school text has yet been tried on an extensive scale by teachers co-operating with linguists, and it would seem evident that this is both an important and a fruitful area for experimentation. Since the newer grammarians emphasize approaching the language as a totality and insist on describing it in terms of pattern and form, their point of view should be of considerable value in relating discussions of style in composition or literature with the formal study of language.

In fact, there should be no essential quarrel between the traditionalists and the modernists in this sphere, for both insist on the formal study of grammar and both are committed to analysing and describing the language. When a modernist insists on a more rigorous kind of definition and a more consistent type of description, he is asking not for a revolution but a refinement of principles. The newer linguistic approaches, when they do become a part of the school programme, will occupy the same kind of relation to English studies of the past as the newer mathematics occupies to the arithmetic of the past. Neither contradicts what has been done but rather both place it on a firmer theoretical basis.

Apart from grammatical studies there is a considerable need for careful investigation of other areas of formal language study. Now that the languages of advertising and public relations have become so important, the area of semantics seems of increasing relevance in the English programme. How meaning is structured, how words change meaning, how changes in context change meaning are topics of vital importance to the student today. Here again the contemporary linguist, psychologist, and anthropologist have a good deal to contribute to the study of English. There is considerable necessity for further study and refinement of teaching in this area, both as a preventive measure against the misuse of language for manipulative purposes in politics, news transmission, and business activities and as a guide in increasing a student's powers of expression and composition.

Closely allied to semantics and relating English to mathematics, is the subject of logic. As part of their language study all high-school students should be given some formal training in logic and in the application of logic to the study of language. The introduction of mathematical logic into the mathematics departments will have an indirect effect on the study of English, for it will no longer be possible to consider only the traditional logic. The value of transfer from the study of mathematics to the study of language and literature should certainly be exploited by the teacher of English. Since, however, this too is a new approach, investigation and study are needed to develop a programme for achieving these ends.

Each of the aspects of formal language study has relations to the study of literature as well. Word-building, for example, not only increases vocabulary, but also tells a student something about word meaning, various forms of rhyme, and other aspects of poetry. Semantics is valuable in dealing with ambiguity, irony, and problems of meaning in poetry, prose, and the drama. Grammar provides ways of speaking about different kinds of stylistic devices and a basis for a treatment of rhetoric which is one possible kind of approach to the study of literary structure.

Each of the sections of formal language study has relevance to different levels of the school programme. Grammar in the early grades, for example, may have to do with the intuitive understanding of certain dominant patterns which a child develops. In the later grades of elementary school, it may have to do with the recognition of certain major kinds of words—word classes which have concrete manifestations in structure, such as the inflection of nouns and verbs for number. In high school it moves into a broader understanding of the abstract patterns of language at various levels, devices of subordination, government, concord and the like, as well as the abstract patterns of over-all English structure.

It is probably not adequately realized that the first grammar lesson begins at an early stage in the first grade reading programme before a child has ever heard the word "grammar" mentioned. In a similar way the first lesson in semantics begins in the pre-primer stage when a child studies the problem of context. Since these are not usually recognized as goals of the programme at this level, there is certainly a necessity for a study of the influence the early reader has on a child's grasp of the formal structure of his language or the influence of the reading-readiness programme on his approach to semantic problems. The formal principles of language study probably should play a much larger role in the organization of this part of the programme. It is interesting, therefore, to note that semanticists and linguists such as I. A. Richards, Henry Lee Smith, and even Leonard Bloomfield himself have actively interested themselves in the design of first-grade reading programmes.

Beyond the schools, formal language study should become an even more central part of a student's programme. In university a student should be exposed to courses in the history of the language and its structure and linguistic make-up at different points in its history. The future teacher should have a grasp of the history of the language, its present structure and its structure at various periods in the past. Furthermore she or he should come into contact with some of the general principles of linguistics, semantics, and other parts of language study.

In many ways this is one of the most challenging sections of English studies for future development. Nothing can be duller or more lifeless than inadequate formal language study. Yet nothing can be more thrilling than this subject when it is properly taught. The present state of the formal study of language in the schools would seem to justify a major reconsideration of the methods of instruction, the integration of divisions of the subject, the early introduction of the structure of the language in reading and other experiences. Some correlation should be developed between the teaching of composition , literature, and language and between the newer programme in mathematics and the introduction of logic into the English programme. Such a study would examine the ways in which the newer linguistic approach to grammar could be incorporated into the school programme and the ways in which the naivety that Firth and others have attacked could be eliminated.

Since the development of most of the knowledge that is involved in the study of the nature and structure of the language has been so rapid in the past decades, it would seem advisable to provide various kinds of in-course training for teachers. An experimental programme would need to include some kind of seminar for participating teachers to exchange ideas and to study the principles involved in the programme. Furthermore, with the growing importance of this area, it is essential that teachers receive in teachers' colleges and universities far more extensive preparation in the studies that are important to the teaching of the English language.

6. ENGLISH IN GRADE 13

Taking a swing at Grade 13 seems to be the most popular current educational exercise; whether the process is strengthening or enervating is not altogether clear. This committee wishes to dissociate itself from such general condemnation as "neither a good preparation for university nor a valuable educational experience," but it does not accept the proposition that the Grade 13 courses and examinations are either above criticism or beyond the sphere of responsibility of classroom teachers. Although the tone of much of this section of the report is critical of existing practices, the members of the committee are convinced that much excellent work is being done both by students and by teachers of Grade 13, and that the best students are at least as well prepared for university as they have ever been.

The basic difficulty lies not so much in the courses or even the examinations, but in the enormous importance attached to the results of the Departmental examinations in June. These results tend to be the main factor in judging the success of a student's whole high-school career, his eligibility for admission to university or any form of further education, his chances for employment, the reputation of the school from which he comes, and the efficiency of individual teachers in that school. This situation, except in the case of unusually independent and perceptive students and teachers, leads to a concentration on the memorizing of examinable material and corresponding neglect of the genuine search for truth and knowledge which is the basis of all real education.

The committee supports the belief that all Grade 13 students should be required to study English. At this stage, however, the problem of whether all students should take the same course becomes particularly thorny. For the student with literary ability and taste the study of English should be not only a delight, but a rigorous and demanding discipline. The sort of teaching which would most benefit him is obviously not suited to the student whose tastes and abilities lie in a different direction. Fortunately the nature of the subject-matter provides some amelioration, but the attempt to steer a middle course can and does frequently result in a dull, plodding, factual approach which leads to first class honours and frustration for the good student and to boredom and a credit for most of the others. It may be that Grade 13 students are taught so well, or at least so carefully, that they fail to develop the capacity for self-reliance and self-discipline which is essential to success at the university.

The basis for the course in English composition is the writing of essays. If this results in encouraging a student to become well informed about important matters of academic or general interest, to learn to organize his ideas and marshal them in logical fashion, and to set them down with some degree of clarity, cogency, wit, and grace, then the value of such training is beyond doubt. But if, as is too frequently the case, he is being taught a superficial kind of skill in the handling of a mode of writing which is essentially artificial for him, then the value of the training is highly questionable. The problem of the kind of writing which would best test and develop the student's ability to handle language needs careful review.

Most teachers are agreed that the writing of *précis* is a valuable exercise in comprehension, analysis, and synthesis. Some confusion still exists about the relationship of *précis* to paraphrase, but Departmental policy in this matter is now fairly clear.

Practice in translation from foreign languages into idiomatic English is excellent training in composition, but there is less opportunity for developing this facility than there used to be and sometimes the benefit is lost by the student's being required to memorize long stretches of arid prose.

The range of vocabulary within the reach of most Grade 13 students is pitifully narrow. The best remedy for this, of course, is wide reading, but the student at this stage may complain with some justice that he simply has not time for reading outside his courses of study.

The so-called "prose appreciation" part of the course seems to have been

improved in the past few years by the substitution of more specific questions for the previous invitation to display a knowledge of critical terms
without really understanding their operation or effect.

The inept and ineffective use of language in answer papers on subjects
other than English Composition poses the question whether the present
form of examination in that subject provides a satisfactory means of
testing the student's ability to write. Certainly, substituting objective-type
questions for the writing of continuous prose seems likely to do more harm
than good, but surely a close and intelligent study could result in improvement in the present system.

The course in literature is built around five main literary genres: drama,
poetry, the novel, the essay, and the short story. Since the Shakespeare
play is in verse, the result is that about three-quarters of the teaching time
is spent on poetry. This is not necessarily a defect, but does suggest a
problem of balance which calls for consideration.

Most teachers seem to agree that the Shakespeare study is the most
satisfactory part of the course. This supports the committee's theory that
the best material is likely to provide the best education and the greatest
satisfaction. But even Shakespeare can be made dull if teachers and
students pursue this aim with determination. The question most frequently
raised concerning the study of Shakespeare is whether a single play is
enough. This, in turn, raises the broader question of the relative value of
intensive and extensive study. There are obvious advantages in each
approach. The depth and subtlety of Shakespeare provide the perfect
opportunity for intensive study, but the experiment of reading several
plays would certainly be interesting and probably enlightening.

The other part of the course in drama is less satisfactory. The committee
approves the idea of having a "modern" play as a complement to one by
Shakespeare, but the differences in difficulty and quality in the plays
selected from year to year present a real problem. To devote an equal
amount of time, for example, to *Murder in the Cathedral* and *The Heiress*
seems a rather curious approach to the study of literature.

The committee is somewhat sceptical of the value of dividing poetry
into longer and shorter poems, especially since the "shorter" poems are
sometimes longer than the "longer" ones. There is also a problem of time
involved. Study of the "shorter" poems takes a much larger share of the
teaching time than would seem justified by the marks allotted to this part
of the course, but it is very difficult to make a satisfactory study of a sonnet,
for example, in less than a full period. There is the further question of
whether the student might not benefit more from selections made with

some sort of rationale or pattern of approach in mind. Designing of several experimental courses on this basis might prove rewarding. The teaching of poetry probably provides the severest test of the teacher's skill and understanding; more help from experienced and successful teachers for the young non-specialists is particularly needed in this area.

The novel provides an obvious opportunity to experiment with techniques for extensive study, particularly, perhaps, on a comparative basis. The advent of the paperback book has made the inclusion of four or five novels in the course quite a practical possibility, providing that the Department and teachers of English are willing to try new approaches and modify examinations accordingly.

The chief weakness of the short story and essay part of the course is the narrow range of material now examined. This is more important in connection with the essay than with the short story, because the genre is so inclusive and because much of the prose of thought is the sort of thing which the student is likely to be required to write in one way or another for the rest of his life. A study of many different kinds of essays and of different prose styles should be of great benefit to his own prose style. There is, of course, a danger of moving too far in this direction and emphasizing style at the expense of content, but the present emphasis seems too heavily weighted in the opposite direction. Perhaps a better balance might be achieved through judicious experiment.

In the whole field of the study of English literature, but especially at the Grade 13 level, the value of a good school library cannot be overstressed. At this stage the student should be doing a good deal of his work independently and a large and carefully chosen selection of books is essential both to the technique and to the attitude required for this sort of study.

The committee finds three main weaknesses in the examination in literature. First, the examination is too long (or the time of writing too short); second, the paper is divided into too many questions, parts of questions, and subdivisions of parts; third, it is frequently not clear to a student just what the examiner wants to know or how much he wants to know about it.

A student who excels in mathematics is able not only to get correct solutions, but to get them more quickly than his less able or less knowledgeable colleagues. Almost the exact reverse is true of literature. The more a student knows about a question (providing the question is really worth asking), the more complex and time-consuming is the process of marshalling his knowledge, making his selection of the most relevant material, organizing it into a logical and convincing argument, and setting down his ideas in effective fashion. If it is necessary to examine on the whole course, perhaps it would be possible to prepare a section of the paper which would test, in a series of short factual answers which could be assessed with a high degree of objectivity as correct or incorrect, whether the student had covered the course. Having demonstrated this, he could then go on to answer two or three more penetrating questions designed to find out whether he knew anything about literature.

The fragmentation of an examination paper into twenty or more small parts is surely a design better fitted to correspond to a detailed marking-scheme than to test the power of a student's appreciation of literature. It seems to defeat rather than aid an attempt to bring a candidate's full powers of thought to bear on a significant literary issue. When to this is added the fact that no indication of the value of the answer expected is given on the question paper and that the point of a question not infrequently rests on a word which is unfamiliar or has a particular connotation in the context, the odds against the student mount significantly. Under these circumstances it should not be a complete surprise to have even relatively intelligent students write shallow and occasionally stupid answers.

Perhaps the biggest problem of all in connection with the examination is to get the necessary number of competent people to give the time required to deal with the annual avalanche of papers. The problem applies equally to chief examiners, committee members, and associate examiners. That the present situation is not satisfactory is attested by many experienced and able teachers who have found that relatively poor students often get marks much higher than they really deserve, and, less frequently, that good students are down a grade, or even two, from where they should be.

It has been suggested from time to time that the solution to this problem may be found in taking over the techniques employed by either the Americans or the British, i.e., the examinations of the College Entrance Board, or those for the General Certificate of Education. The committee does not regard this as a happy solution and calls attention to the fact that both of these examinations are being called seriously in question in their countries of origin. Nor does the suggestion that the Grade 13 examination be moved back to Grade 12 seem to us to have much merit; indeed, the situation might well be made worse instead of better. If an examination is not satisfactory for Grade 13, it is hardly likely to be better for Grade 12. Moreover, the additional number of candidates involved would place an even greater strain on administrative machinery already creaking under its present load. It seems to us that both the philosophy and the mechanics of Grade 13 courses and examinations need a thorough study, and that it should be undertaken as soon as possible.

7. THE UNIVERSITY AND THE ENGLISH PROGRAMME

This report has dealt more fully with the elementary and secondary levels of education, because it is at these levels that all students encounter English as a major part of the curriculum. At the university level, however, specialization begins so early that it excludes English from a major role in the studies of students who are not pursuing an arts course. In spite of this fact, the committee feels that there are certain aspects of the university programme in English that demand attention. First, the committee feels that all students attending university should be required to do some work in English, preferably one or two years. Certainly such a course should be required of all students planning a career in teaching, since they may be required to teach English as well as their special subjects at some point during their teaching careers. Furthermore, if the proper humanistic spirit is to inform the society that the schools serve, it is important that some continuing contact with the study of language and literature be maintained by students in professional and scientific courses.

One reason for the rather extensive failure of English courses in these areas and therefore possibly an indirect reason for much of the hostility towards the arts course on the part of some professional and scientifically trained people, is the fact that too often instruction in these courses is provided by young graduate students who have not taught before and have had little or no guidance in how to handle a class. If the university is to continue its empirical tradition of allowing young, inexperienced, graduate students to practise the art of teaching on their first classes, it is probably advisable that these classes be composed of senior students in the general arts programme who will profit from the enthusiasm and energy of the novice teacher without suffering from his lack of experience in teaching. First year classes and especially terminal classes in the sciences and professional schools might profitably be taught by the most experienced and mature members of the academic staff who can be guaranteed to impart both knowledge and respect for humanistic studies.

The committee also feels that there are some changes which might profitably be considered in the structure of the university curriculum. The committee queries whether or not the purely historical approach is effective, or whether or not an approach providing courses in literary types, critical methods, individual writers, literary theory, and historical periods would produce a more balanced scholar and teacher upon graduation. Certainly the imparting of a knowledge of the structure of modern English grammar should have as high priority in the university programme as the provision of courses in Anglo-Saxon. In the first year of the university programme, a course in contemporary drama, novel, or essay, might be more profitable than a study of the Renaissance. In fact, the whole question of historical treatment might be approached inductively, beginning with the modern period and working backwards, rather than beginning with the earlier periods and working up to the contemporary. While it has no specific recommendation, the committee feels that some experimentation with the university curriculum might provide a more fruitful education for the students who are to become the teachers of the future. Certainly a teacher who knows nothing of contemporary writing or the structure of modern English is not going to find Anglo-Saxon an effective aid in the secondary school classroom. Members of the committee thought that a course such as literary criticism would be particularly valuable to students planning to follow a career in the teaching of English and that such a course should be in the form of a seminar coming close to the end of the undergraduate programme. They also felt that courses in practical criticism, rhetorical analysis, and the reading of texts, might well be part of the initial training in English at the university level. The question of breadth in the programme for a future English teacher is also important. It is probably worth considering that many teachers believe that a course in Philosophy and English or English and History is often superior to the honour English course, which may well suffer from over-specialization.

Apart from the English course, committee members thought that the studies of a student desiring to teach English after graduation might be designed to include some of the following elements: Classics in Translation, or Classics; non-European literature in translation (especially Oriental and Far Eastern literature); music; art, or aesthetics. In fact, the committee's insistence generally on the presence of a wider range of artistic education in the schools suggests that, at university, future teachers should receive training in the interrelationship of the arts and perhaps in some art other than literature.

Teachers should be encouraged to do work at the graduate level. A graduate course is often considered to be more immediately useful for classroom teaching than undergraduate courses, and the scholarly discipline of the graduate course often seems to provide both stimulus and precision for the practising teacher. The pursuit of an M.A. degree is considered to be of value to every teacher since it provides considerable training, is excellent for developing intellectual discipline, and increases sensitivity. It should be apparent, however, that not all kinds of M.A. projects are equally useful to a teacher and that the graduate school faculty should keep in mind the requirements of a teaching career when guiding practising teachers, or future teachers, in their M.A. work. A B.A. thesis is not considered by the committee as particularly useful in these respects.

There is no reason for thinking that the education of a teacher must cease with the M.A. degree. It should be of value both for the discipline and for the individual if a teacher pursues a programme of doctoral studies. There are, however, problems involved which need careful study. Are not some programmes of doctoral studies so specialized as to preclude the participation of anyone who is not exclusively interested in pursuing a highly technical form of scholarship? Similarly, are not many theses projects of such a nature as to interfere with the teacher's broad humanistic development in their insistence on a close, technical, specialized approach to a narrow or limited problem? Since higher graduate studies will increasingly be involved in the training of teachers as well as of research scholars, there is necessity for re-examination of principles and practice at this level, to provide a Ph.D. programme which will meet all of the needs that it should be expected to serve.

The committee feels that to bolster up a university effort to improve training of future teachers, schools of education might well require a minimum number of English courses from all future teachers, since it is well known that English is one of the subjects most frequently taught by non-specialists. Such a requirement would reinforce a university requirement that all students must take one or two years of English. In closing this section, the committee presents in outline form some of the questions that might profitably be asked concerning university programmes in English:

(i) Should university students in all courses and faculties have some sort of instruction in English? ("To fail in Latin or mathematics is to be deficient in those subjects; to fail in English is to be fundamentally uneducated.") Some possibilities are: (*a*) a series of related courses; (*b*) seminars; (*c*) required reading and summer term papers.

(ii) Can more joint courses with other departments be worked out?

(iii) Is there over-emphasis on (*a*) secondary sources; (*b*) lectures which are definitive and become almost course text-books; (*c*) particular periods or writers (e.g., Anglo-Saxon)?

    (iv) Should more be done with: (*a*) linguistics and history of the language; (*b*) theories of literature; (*c*) Philosophy; (*d*) influence of other literatures and cultures; (*e*) relationships among the humanities?

    (v) What kinds of courses should be offered to students in engineering, medicine, etc.?

    (vi) Are examination procedures satisfactory?

    (vii) Can teaching methods be improved?

    (viii) What use can be made of media other than books and lectures?

    (ix) Should there be a course in writing?

8. TEACHER TRAINING

Teachers' training colleges are expected to do the impossible—to produce for the schools devoted teachers with sound backgrounds of knowledge, and with an understanding of boys and girls and of the ways of challenging young minds and encouraging learning. Proverb and parable assure us that figs cannot be made from thistles, or bread from stones; yet training colleges in Ontario have had to admit candidates with limited scholarship and inadequate control of their own language. Until recently it was possible to enter an Ontario teachers' college with standing in *either* English Composition or English literature in the Grade 13 examinations. A pass mark at that stage might have been the only one achieved during the year.

Strains on the schools imposed by increased enrolments have been the justification offered for this leniency in standards of admission. Though this situation is easing, and standards of admission are rising, there are throughout the province numbers of teachers poorly qualified. Unless they are alert and industrious enough to recognize their deficiencies and take steps to remedy them, hundreds of children may suffer. The teaching of English is especially vulnerable, for to this subject a teacher should bring resources of knowledge, taste, sympathy, and imagination, as well as the essential love of books and of words. Incompetence in English goes deeper than the committing of errors in spelling and grammar. The teacher who is to guide children to the appreciation of literature and the improvement of expression cannot afford to be a limited person.

Canada has been slow to recognize officially the need for more thorough preparation of its young teachers for the elementary schools. England, with similar problems of teacher shortage, handles the situation very differently. The training colleges there draw students from holders of the General Certificate of Education at the Advanced Level, and give them three further years of combined academic and professional training. This would amount to a standard roughly equivalent to three years of general arts in an Ontario university plus a year of teacher training.

Obviously, much damage has been done to education in Ontario through the unfortunate lowering of standards. It is time now to raise the requirements sharply. Candidates should be required to approach the teaching profession with as much respect as they would a university or any occupation requiring superior intelligence and skill. Nothing is more distressing to teachers who value their profession than to see indifferent young people choose it as a second or third best. Many fine students now select teaching as a career. No time should be lost in weeding out the undesirables and attracting candidates of quality. With material of high calibre the teachers' colleges will be able to demand a standard of achievement that would rapidly be reflected in the work of children.

Students entering teachers' colleges for either the elementary or the secondary level must have distinguished masters. The prestige of training colleges depends on the calibre of their staffs. The greatest care should be taken to secure men and women of distinguished scholarship, teaching ability, and experience. Great teachers bring to the work that is both vocation and avocation a gift, not easily described, for stirring curiosity and imagination, for making learning exciting, and hard work worth the effort. Such teaching is stimulating and infectious. Its effects can be seen in the intellectual excitement of many classrooms. There can be no better way of attracting promising young teachers to the profession.

The limited period of time now spent at training colleges encourages an emphasis on methods rather than on content. The college can do much by its presentation to make young teachers realize the importance of knowing their subject-matter, of constantly adding to their knowledge, and of understanding that they should know more than they can teach. Every effort should be made to acquaint prospective teachers with ways in which they can enrich their background of reading and improve their powers of expression. The libraries of teachers' colleges at all levels should be libraries of good reading, not merely of pedagogical reference. If, during the year, student teachers have little time for reading, they should at least be exposed to it. Library assignments, lectures on books and book selection, and the provision of book lists should be part of the general curriculum. Teachers of science, history, geography, and mathematics should know the best reference books on English usage as well as the books that are best in their own fields. School and classroom libraries are probably the best material for enriching courses, but too many teachers are at present unaware of the outstanding books in their own fields. In the library the two cultures that C. P. Snow finds such a regrettable feature of modern education can meet.

Prospective teachers in all subjects should have some instruction in the effective use of the voice. Poor enunciation and delivery can mar the best material, in university classrooms as well as in the schools. Teachers of English should be expected to read well, and should be given help if their performance is not adequate. Too little attention has been paid on this continent to the production of clear, effective speakers.

The content and arrangement of courses in English at training colleges should be examined carefully and the emphasis on various parts of the courses weighed. Too heavy an emphasis on the technical aspects of teaching reading may result in an ignoring of literary values. For some limited young teachers all selections are problems in reading. Teachers in training for the high schools often find poetry emphasized for much of the year to the virtual exclusion of prose. The result is that they are at a loss when asked to discuss an essay or a short story.

There is great need for a re-assessment of the methods that have dominated classrooms at various stages of education. The Socratic question-and-answer method used almost exclusively in secondary school classrooms leads to the treatment of literature in neat but artificial segments, and often limits the practice of writing. Students in training expect to teach a lesson with a beginning, a middle, and an end. It is essential that they be able to handle such lessons, but the cost in educational values may be heavy. Pupils might often be reading or writing instead of marching through the inevitable pattern.

Teachers of composition in the training colleges could greatly assist the teaching of the subject in schools by using their classes of teachers in training as the equivalent of a class of pupils in school. The "pupils" could be taken through a course in composition, provided with the stimulus for writing, and in turn expected to produce sample compositions to be read and evaluated by their classmates. Some of the ways of evoking good writing could thus be discovered, and the need for form, discipline, and revision could be emphasized. Problems of improving expression could be handled as in an actual classroom. Teachers might become writers.

All teachers in training should have a general view of a child's progress and of the various stages in his development, with some appreciation of the ways in which he can be encouraged or retarded.

An imaginative programme of in-service training has been urged in other sections of this report. Many teachers learn with their pupils. Given interest and will, an impoverished reading background can be enriched, and a love of books cultivated. Well-stocked libraries teach teachers as well as pupils. Any community with imagination and enterprise can secure talented speakers to spark the desire to improve, or to lead discussion groups. Outstanding teachers can be released from their classrooms and used to give demonstrations and to speak to groups of novices. One of the greatest wastes in education has been the failure to use such talent wisely.

9. THE ENGLISH TEACHER, THE POPULAR ARTS, AND THE MEDIA

The rapid growth of new media of communication and the wider dissemination of popular art forms in print, film, television, radio, and the phonograph have posed peculiar problems for the twentieth-century teacher. Investigation of the effect of this revolution in communications on the teaching process is still in an embryonic state, but it is generally apparent that it is of considerable significance to any group engaged in teaching either language or the arts. One of the major reasons for the teaching of criticism to secondary school and university students is that such training develops the ability to analyse and assess the popular arts and the manipulative techniques of advertisers and communicators. Since modern attention to design has taught the rhetoric of form to all of these areas of activity, it is vitally important to provide students with the proper kind of equipment to protect themselves. It is equally important that a student be aware of the fact that he carries on different levels of activity for different reasons. To watch "Checkmate" on television for entertainment, but with awareness that the plots are stock and trite, is far better than to confuse "Checkmate" with the serious dramatic endeavour of "Festival" on CBC. Criticism is not only important because it carries over to the assessment of such programmes, but because it enables a student to apply the same techniques to handicrafts, fashions, the shape of the city in which he lives, and, in fact, his entire life.

The powerful effect of these media has a twofold significance for a teacher of English. The first and most important question has to do with the understanding of the media, the second and less important, with the use of the media in the educational process. The first question has been the subject of a recent report by Professor Marshall McLuhan to the

United States Office of Education. This report, *Understanding Media*, emphasizes the importance of teaching an understanding of the new media at the secondary-school level. Certainly this function should concern departments of English, for it is intimately involved with the kind of aesthetic problems that are the function of an English teacher. The radio, the musical comedy, the television programme, represent different uses of the language with different kinds of decorum. The type of language used in a serious report, in a discussion programme on television, in a television drama, in a radio drama, and in stage drama has of necessity to be different. If the use of language and the manipulation of form in such areas are not to become irresponsible, it is important that they receive the kind of humanistic attention that the writing of letters, compositions, poems, and the like have always received. Furthermore, the various media themselves pose problems of form, since they impose special and different kinds of form on materials. While this area is new and growing, it seems to this committee that it provokes the kind of question in need of more extensive investigation and research. The McLuhan report is tentative and generalized. Study of the area must be developed in a fuller and more sophisticated manner, but it is vital that this be the province of a teacher of humanities, for the function and use of these forms are primarily humanistic.

This question overlaps with the second question, the teaching of English through the use of these new media. Here again the problem is partly knowing what each of the various media has to contribute to the teaching function. Possibly phonograph records are better tools for poetry instruction, and television or films for dramatic instruction. Possibly limited use of films or television can be made for the teaching of poetry, but it is certainly important in such uses to recognize the rather central differences between poetry written for recitation, poetry written for the printed page, poetry written for illustration, and poetry written for dramatic performance. Students must likewise become aware of these rather important differences. A sense of the complexity of language may easily be harmed by visual presentation of poetry just as much as it may be assisted. In teaching poetry by such methods, it is important that the teacher be fully aware of what he or she is doing. Some film strips that have been used to teach great works of literature may do more to damage literary interest and response than all the difficulties encountered when reading the poem in an unattractive edition.

One aspect of these media which cannot be too heavily emphasized is the importance of having large enough budgets available. Such associations as the (American) Council for a Television Course in the Humanities have established educational leadership in this area by refusing to compromise educational effectiveness by the contingencies of a limited budget. Educational television, to be respectable, must be of the highest quality; if it does not have this quality it should not be countenanced. This is just as true of educational films, or any other materials prepared for educational purposes. The average teacher or school board would object to having important text-books cut in quantity or quality for the mere reason of budget. If the other forms of disseminating information are to come of age in the educational world, a similar uncompromising, professional attitude is necessary. It should be an embarrassment to all teachers to compare the amount of skill and effort put forth in televising the average light entertainment with that given to the various attempts at educational television.

The very existence of such a situation as that posed by the mass media requires a reconsideration of the entire programme of the humanities. The film, the radio, the television set, not only provide the context within which language and literature must be taught, but they also provide techniques for changing the values of language and literature. It is of the utmost importance for teachers to understand the transformation of a work as it moves from one media to another. What are the results of such transformations in individual experience and what is the pervasive effect of many such transformations on the community of the arts? These questions are in need of extensive investigation and can only be answered by the mutual participation of teachers and people experienced with the varied media. Projects such as those carried out by the CBC's school broadcasts and children's entertainment divisions and proposals for joint American–Canadian series in the humanities for secondary schools bring together academically trained people and specialists in the media of television in a context which provides for consideration of these problems. The continuation of such projects in conjunction with general study of curriculum is to be encouraged and might well become another feature of the experimental programmes suggested in this report.

10. CONCLUSION

This commentary on the teaching of English has considered some of the most significant aspects of the subject, and the implications of these at various stages of the child's development. Its treatment has, of necessity, been general and over-simplified. Despite the use of section headings, the report has emphasized the essential unity of English studies. The assumption that education is a continuous process would seem to lead naturally to the development of a sequential programme that would add breadth and depth to the student's knowledge of the English language and its literature. The theorist may see in his mind's eye a printed curriculum that, if followed, would produce a generation of children growing steadily in proficiency with language, and storing their minds with the best that has been said and thought.

The curriculum is at best, however, a design to be interpreted by teachers, for children—by teachers with varying degrees of ability and insight, for children with differing equipment in intelligence and language background. In raising the question of the possibility of sequential programmes in English, the committee would warn against a neat formula, or any interpretation that might result in a rigid curriculum with a lock-step treatment. The ideas of sequence and integration should be interpreted broadly, to give reasonable freedom to individual school systems and schools. Indeed, no other approach is suitable for this subject.

The inductive method implied by Bruner's book, *The Process of Education*, would seem to be appropriate for the study of English, since it promises the interest and excitement of a first response, the focussing of attention through observation, and the intellectual challenge of drawing conclusions from what has been read, heard, or observed. Probably this is the natural way of responding to new experiences in reading, writing, and language study. Most skilled teachers use this method, but with more thoughtful selection and greater emphasis it might provide a wider range of reading, adding depth in the increasing awareness of form, and in appreciation of the resources of language as a means of expression. Research and experiment with this approach, and with that suggested in the essay on rhetoric, would require a series of investigations, some beginning immediately in a small way, others demanding long-term study and planning.

All the committee's discussions have returned to the teacher as the centre of the English programme. No revision of curriculum will produce satisfactory results unless there is a continued effort to encourage people with intelligence, knowledge, sympathy, and imagination to undertake the teaching. Ingenious methods are no substitute for the talented teacher. Refreshment and in-service training for those already teaching are among the major recommendations of this report.

The committee recognizes the differing degrees of intelligence, aptitude, and language background that children bring with them to school. Much of their education in language takes place through their parents and the mass media. These influences may reinforce or hinder the school's teaching, and are often stronger than the influence of the school. The same type of teaching is not necessarily appropriate for all children, or for advanced students in different types of courses. If full advantage is to be taken of opportunities to improve technical and commercial education, it is essential that gifted, imaginative, and experienced teachers be given the opportunity to experiment with courses and methods. No subject gives greater scope for enrichment than does English. The problem of the external examination is its failure to distinguish between various purposes and emphases. Consideration of revised curricula requires consideration of examinations not as ends in themselves, but as part of the process of education. The shifting of an external examination from Grade 13 to Grade 12 is thus no neat solution for an educational programme.

In its investigations the committee has been impressed by the methods used in teaching children to read, but has found itself raising many questions about early reading texts. These questions have been echoed by some people who have made careful studies of the teaching of reading, and by many teachers who feel that reading material should offer more stimulus for the mind of the learner, "a more provocative invitation to intellectual activity," as one critic said. The early readers have long escaped a fundamental examination in terms of content, vocabulary, and sentence patterns. The preparation of new readers is a costly and time-consuming process, but revision is overdue. The bringing together of writers of skill and taste, and advisers with special knowledge of the problems involved, should be an immediate concern of the proper authorities.

The skills of reading, the selections in the readers, and the stories read to him are a child's invitation to explore the richness and variety of the world of books. There can be no better way of spending money for education than by stocking school libraries with the widest possible range of good reading. No school should be handicapped by cramped quarters and inadequate staffing. No community that lacks a library should consider itself complete.

It is important that, in reading, the mind and the imagination be fed early, that reading be regarded as more than a process, and that a young reader be offered fare richer than the abridgment stripped of its colour by too rigidly controlled vocabulary. For too many children the study of literature depends too strongly and for too long on anthologies. The committee welcomes the flood of paper-back books that offers for young people the possibility of more extensive reading. Equally welcome are the signs of a restoration to favour for young children of fairy-tale and folk-tale, myth and legend. The committee would urge that immediate experiments be undertaken in the building of sequential reading programmes to increase the range and depth of reading. The object should be not a limited list of titles, but, as the Modern Language Association pamphlet suggests, lists that investigate different kinds of stories, and different ways of treating narrative; recurring themes treated in different ways; the many resources of a given form. The enjoyment, even the delight, of discovery can be deepened by an increasing awareness of the writer's art, and by the building of a substantial store of reading.

The members of the committee are agreed that the study of language is necessary, that it must be closely related to speech and writing, to classes in reading, and to the study of effective prose. In this period of transition in language study it is essential that teachers be informed of the type of work being done by linguists. Though their investigations have not yet produced material available in form suitable for day-by-day teaching, the new concepts and methods should be assessed by schools and universities. Study and experiment are needed to indicate the most economical and effective ways of giving students a firm grasp of the basic forms of standard usage. At present much time and effort are wasted in repetition. Investigations in a sequential programme may result in greater control of standard usage, of punctuation, of the structure of sentence, paragraph, and continuous prose. In the interrelationship of reading, writing, and language study lies the firm foundation of English as a subject.

11. RECOMMENDATIONS

(i) That long-term studies and experiments in the shaping of sequential programmes in English be undertaken by groups representing all stages of education in the schools and the university.

(ii) That a careful review of existing early readers be followed by the preparation of new readers, the committees in charge to include linguists, psychologists, teachers, and experts in design, to assist and advise the writers.

(iii) That libraries and library facilities be regarded as an essential part of *all* schools, both elementary and secondary, and that library service be extended to provide adequate materials for reference problems and recreational reading.

(iv) That experimental programmes in literature be undertaken in individual schools and classrooms, and that the results of the experiments be made available to all teachers.

(v) That the timetables of the various grades be reviewed to ensure adequate attention to all aspects of English, and that in this review, courses in speech and drama be considered as part of the English programme.

(vi) That the reading of the intermediate grades be reinforced by longer selections, including appropriate novels.

(vii) That a long-term study of grammar and language teaching be begun, accompanied by classroom demonstration, and discussion with teachers.

(viii) That an in-service programme for the teaching of writing be initiated, using lectures, discussion groups, teachers' writing groups, classroom experiments, and demonstrations.

(ix) That arrangements be made for distribution of information about English studies and teaching: book-lists, digests of articles, news of experimental programmes, samples of student writing.

(x) That, in the interests of education as a whole, there be set up a continuing committee to consider and strengthen the relationship between English and other subjects.

(xi) That a continuing committee be established to consider ways of recruiting teachers with suitable qualifications for teaching of English.

(xii) (*a*) That a comprehensive study be made of the impact of the mass media on the teaching of English. (*b*) That a programme to experiment with the use of television and other mass media be set up in selected schools, and that the results of such experiments be made available to teachers.

D. F. THEALL

Apparently, English is, of all school subjects, the most prosaic and the least in need of revision. Yet the experience of the committee proved that it is one of the most important areas for future study and curriculum planning. The field of English, although central, is so accepted that it is apt to be overlooked in any revision study. In fact, it is generally felt that everyone is a specialist in English studies and that there is little that is not already known. This kind of naive confidence denies the fact that knowledge we have possessed is often lost in a practical sense, and that it must be rediscovered. It also denies that education is a formative process, and as such grows and progresses, constantly discovering new frontiers of knowledge. The committee on English found itself constantly led on excursions into new areas of consideration: the interrelationship among the arts; the possibility of a philosophy or science of form; and into other fields of learning, such as the new researches in the psychology of thinking (Bruner, Piaget and Osgood, etc.); the discoveries in linguistics and its allied discipline, semantics; and recent developments in mathematical logic and scientific thought.

The study of English cannot remain isolated from such concerns, because the advancement of knowledge has provided new perspectives of the relationships between these diverse fields and the study of language and literature. In fact, the committee discovered that not only with respect to post-Coleridgean literary criticism, but with respect to virtually all areas that make up the field in English, it is no longer possible to continue, as in the eighteenth century, without an awareness of psychology, the social sciences and the newer discoveries in the sciences. In such circumstances, it is apparent that considerable attention must be given to the ways in which the traditional teaching of English can be adapted to new and changed situations. It cannot be the province of any single observer or small committee of observers to provide the keys that will open the door to orderly change. The present report primarily attempts to document some of the areas in which further study is needed.

If the question of the relationship of English to other subjects in the curriculum is a serious problem, even more serious is the question of whether there is any essential unity in the study of English itself. One of the most promising developments from the point of view of achieving unification within the diverse activities of English studies in the schools is the newly revived interest in the ancient rhetorical tradition. Essentially, English studies have come to replace the study of rhetoric which used classical languages as its foundation. At the heart of the tradition of rhetorical studies was the realization that speech was the primary act of language on the part of man. Rhetorical training was understood as the training of speakers, and hence as an education emphasizing oral composition. It was also a tradition which produced a large number of great writers. While such a discipline cannot and should not be re-introduced into the school curriculum today, there remains the possibility of adapting it to current needs.

Rhetoric involved itself both with the detailed structure (style) and with the over-all structure of oral and written compositions. Consequently, it provided tools for both literary analysis and composition. Rhetoric provided a bridge between the study of other men's artistic productions and the creation of one's own artistic productions. It took the tools of the grammarian and the logician and applied them to the study of style and structure which should form part of the core of an English curriculum.

The rhythm, grace, harmony, and proportion of English prose are to be found in English speech. The effects of writing are successful only because the reader is simultaneously aware of the fact that the language has a structure of sound which makes the words on the page come to life. Therefore, any programme of English studies must of necessity recognize the primacy of speech in the study of English. A rhetorically integrated programme would begin with such a recognition of the central character of speech. For this reason, it is of vital concern how a child learns to read in the first grade; his entire attitude towards the study of literature can be jeopardized by improper teaching of oral reading. To encourage artificialities in reading will distort the child's response to the printed page. This is just one of the reasons for the necessity of recognizing the primacy of speech in the school curriculum. The history of rhetorical studies suggests that this is the traditional, humanistic way of approaching the problem. Writing in a mass-produced form (print) has existed only since the sixteenth century; the humanistic tradition has existed without mass-produced writing since the worlds of Greece and Rome.

Rhetoric as conceived in this report would have value both for the curriculum and for the training of teachers, for it would provide the keys for a successful structuring of the elementary school curriculum as well as permitting the development of a spiral-type curriculum in the study of English. Rhetorical study would indicate the kinds of form and structure that are central to the development of English studies. To take a simple example, it would demonstrate how the concept of sentence pattern is introduced in the first grade reader and then gradually developed and enriched throughout the school experience of the student. To take another example, it would dictate the method by which sentences for analysis and for composition could be divided into more and more discrete parts as the student becomes more and more sophisticated in his handling of language experience. On a larger scale, it might demonstrate how the concept of a simple story plot can undergo successive modifications until it reaches the complexities of the plots of great novels and dramas. In other words, a rhetorical approach might provide direction in the formative processes of literary education.

The major problems of the teaching of English are usually divided into three areas: the study of language, the study of literature, and the study of composition. Recently, it has become fashionable to recognize a sharp distinction between the teaching of reading and the teaching of literature. It should be apparent that a properly developed programme with a rhetorical orientation would see the essential unity of all of these activities. With such a perspective, it would not be possible to divide reading programmes into two volumes—a reader and a literature book, nor would it be possible to question the relevance of language study to either literary study or the study of writing. The forms and patterns pursued in each of these areas must of necessity reinforce and supplement one another, unless English teachers are to be regarded as the most schizophrenic occupational group in our society. Early reading, for example, becomes the first means of teaching a child the patterns of composition as well as the patterns of literature. As soon as the child is made aware of different strategies for achieving the same goal of linguistic communication, he or she has begun to study English.

The report of the English Study Committee does not pretend to be able to examine in detail the ramifications of looking at the subject of English with this kind of perspective, but it must observe that in this kind of perspective rests the hope for the humanities, and especially English, to adapt to the educational demands of a more and more complex society. What is most important at the moment is to establish the importance of some kind of continuing study of these problems. Such a continuing study would have to examine in some detail the relevance of diverse areas of research to the teaching of English, such as the psychology of thinking and the areas of linguistics and semantics mentioned above.

Along with an increased emphasis on an integrated approach towards the field in English, it is equally important that the relationship between English and other subjects be taken into account. Perhaps most fundamental of all these relationships is that between subjects with an aesthetic dimension. Possibly one of the most damaging attitudes to the proper pursuit of English studies is that art and music are merely "frill" subjects. Art, music, and English are all concerned with the creation of forms that express or communicate intellectual–emotional complexes. Art introduces a student to the language of vision and music to the language of sound; the proper study of these arts is bound to have significant effect on how he regards the nature of creative form. Literature and poetry are bound to be influenced by a poor or inadequate programme in art and music, for it is in these forms that a student will first experience the emotional richness resulting from proportion, rhythm, grace and harmony. If, however, the studies of modern psychologists examining the nature of thought are valid, it is also likely that such a failure to provide the proper kind of "aesthetic education" might well result in a similar failure in the ability to compose. Grace of style cannot be developed in a vacuum and in the current situation there is little likelihood of a child's receiving more than occasional experiences of this type through the mass media.

It is probably important, too, that some attention be given to the problem of establishing the relationships between mathematics and science and the area of English studies. It is apparent that certain principles of structure and form that are developed in mathematics and incidentally in science must have immediate transfer value to the area of English. Extensive research involving continual joint participation of individuals from these various disciplines should be carried out. If the field of English is to maintain the respect of the student, it must necessarily take into account legitimate advances and changes in other academic areas.

Since most theorists of literature and most language theorists are in fundamental agreement in stressing such conceptions as form, pattern, structure and the like, it would seem that the study of language and literature could be organized around such a set of principles. It also would seem that the introduction of analytical disciplines such as grammar or literary analysis is quite in keeping with the nature of the subject-matter. Contemporary linguistics has made significant advances in examining the language from the point of view of its formal structure. This applies to the study of writing as well as to the study of speech, although, of necessity, the linguists have stressed the fundamental importance of speech. Linguists, however, do not write school text-books and there is a great need for the collaboration of linguists, English teachers, and educators in the provision of proper texts in the area of modern English grammar. Such texts would provide an important element of an integrated programme of English. Linguistics to the degree that it is, as it professes to be, the objective study of the nature and structure of language, must be of intrinsic interest to all people involved in designing courses of study in English. The field of linguistics would not only make its own contributions to the subject-matter of the school programme, but also should make a significant contribution to its structure. No reader, for example, should be designed without the collaboration of people who are specialists in the areas of linguistics, psychology, and literary theory, and of teachers of children in the particular age groups. One or two men working alone would not attempt to construct an apartment house or an automobile. Isn't there far less justification for their constructing an elementary programme of studies?

One of the major contemporary disputes in the area of English is the battle between the traditional grammarians and the linguists. Such a battle is, in its essence, absurd, for both traditional grammarians and linguists are presumably interested in the same thing and, in fact, traditional grammarians have always regarded themselves as linguists. What is important is that language study in the school be *regarded* as important, and as a subject that can be taught with some degree of sophistication. In view of the alarming fracas between opposing groups, further study of the curriculum problems involved in language study is seriously needed. It should be apparent that the handling or mis-handling of language training in the schools may well result in assisting or damaging the programme in modern languages in the schools and universities. Furthermore, if the field of English can be integrated around the rhetorical approach, it is fundamental that there be a firm cornerstone of language study. It certainly is most often stressed that English teachers must be the guardians of the language in the contemporary world and protect students against misuses of the language. In order to guard against bad grammar or modern corruptions of the language (viz., "advertising" usages), a teacher must provide a student with an extensive and thorough training in the nature of language.

It might seem that so far we have stressed only the formal aspects of the field of English and could be charged with disregarding the emotional experiences, the spiritual values, or the intellectual nourishment with which it is usually associated. This is far from the truth. Such a position as we have expounded above merely recognizes that those values, like all values, must be earned. The deepest emotional experiences, the most profound spiritual values, the keenest and sharpest intellectual visions can only result from persistent study of language and literature. A rhetorical integration for a programme in English would lead to an interest not merely in the textural qualities of style, but also in style in a broader structural sense. The way a character is constructed is in the ultimate analysis a question of style and, therefore, it is a question of style that leads to a demonstration for a reader of what a certain character is like and what attitudes he manifests. A somewhat simple example of such a character might be developed from Mr. Collins, in Jane Austen's *Pride and Prejudice*, and it is, of course, important to note that the characters of *Pride and Prejudice* have different personalities because they speak differently.

A literary work has an extremely complex structure, but in teaching it there must be an attempt to realize that structure and communicate it to students. The lyric poem is so difficult and the novel so easy to teach not solely because students like stories and don't understand lyric poems, but partly because they can read the novel for some kind of effect without ever realizing its literary values, while they cannot read the poem in that manner. Consciously or unconsciously, a writer has nothing more than the range of oral and visual patterns in his language with which to create effects on the reader. Any definition of literature or approach towards literature that blunts this primary truth is bound to have dangerous effects on the study of literature. Literature, along with the other arts and along with life itself, is bound to increase experience and to teach a sense of tragedy and triumph, but its uniqueness is in handling this kind of experience in a medium which is most intimately associated with the life of the intellect— language. It is by now a fairly common admission that much of the sense of triumph and tragedy in Shakespeare, Donne, or Pope cannot be realized unless close attention is paid to their handling of language and structure. Without this kind of attention, Pope now becomes to the reader a popular exponent of deism when he is trying to write a traditional Christian poem that involves a comedy of ideas. How radically the sense of triumph, the joy of comedy suffered from the kind of linguistic ineptness that defined the pun as the lowest form of humour! Our education in English still suffers from a lack of attention to the laughing side of the world. The comic perspective, however, is most likely to depend upon a close structural organization and to involve itself in techniques of irony and surprising verbal and logical arrangement. Yet the range of tragic emotions, too, is deepened considerably by complex interplay within its structure. Students studying *Hamlet*, for example, ought to be able to suggest how and why the speech of Hamlet, Polonius, Claudius, and the other characters differs. How is the effect of Ophelia's madness achieved in terms of structure?

Human values can only be discovered in reality and the reality of literature is the most intellectual reality of man's existence—human language. Consequently, such a close attention to language must always be found at the heart of any curriculum of English. If moral values are part of the province of the teacher of English, they are so because the teacher of English provides an increased sensitivity toward the communicative powers of human language.

Literature is ultimately, as all English teachers want to make it, everything; but unless like all arts it is tied up within its own limits, it can become nothing. The greatest danger in the current teaching of English in the schools is the tendency to stress what literature is in such terms as to make it the same as history, philosophy, the other arts and life itself. Yet traditions of English literature have always realized it is more than that—it is the art (or arts) of the language itself and provides deep insight into the mind and heart of man.

Up to this point, most of the suggestions of this report have been advanced with a particular theoretical basis for the teaching of language and literature in mind. This is not the only theoretical basis possible, but it is one. It has been chosen for the foregoing remarks because it seems to be one of the most useful theoretical frameworks currently available to the teacher. The difference between this kind of approach and a good deal of random activity carried on in changes of curriculum or methodology in English teaching is that there is a firm theoretical foundation and the structure of the subject emanates from that central foundation. One of the prime reasons for extensive and continuing research is the need to try experimentally different kinds of programmes with different theoretical orientations and to discover their relative success or failure in achieving the humanistic goals of the study of English. Such a research programme would have to have the participation of university, high school, and elementary school English teachers and would require a number of experimental schools. The cost of such a project would not be prohibitive if schools already in existence were used on an experimental basis to develop different programmes focussing on different theories of language and literature.

The observations that have been made in this appendix, while suggesting lines that such a study might take, also provide the kind of questions that such a study might test. Is integration of the various aspects of the programme desirable and along what lines? Is the vision of a rhetorical integration a successful one and therefore a means of restoring the complexity of traditional humanistic studies? The sympathies of the committee would favour an affirmative answer; the testing of such a hypothesis awaits the development of the programme and the opportunity to attempt an experimental study of the programme. Such a programme could only be carried out in the same manner as that suggested by the various groups associated with the Modern Language Association in developing their analysis of the problem of an "articulated curriculum." That is, the programme would have to involve in-training, and seminars at the university level for teachers and professors. It would have to involve joint university–school direction of a substantial number of experimental schools within a certain jurisdictional area and ideally it might involve two or three such units working on different kinds of programmes.

The need for adapting English to an entirely new kind of cultural situation in which even the traditional values surrounding the printed page have been altered demands careful study of the role of English studies. With competing media providing obvious artistic contributions, what is the value of literature? Certainly teachers of English are committed to the values of literature, but if they cannot articulate these values in the face of other media, then these values surely will die. Furthermore, what is a teacher's own responsibility to his classes and his subject with respect to the newer forms of communication? A play on television is not merely a play presented by television—it is a television play. For some time there has been a failure to recognize the fundamental differences between the film version of a drama, the drama as read in class, and the drama itself. This cannot continue without serious disruption to the drama. The various media are potential new art forms and as such are an intrinsic part of the humanistic inheritance of man. What is needed is an English programme which approaches the language and literature in such a manner as to permit the student a high degree of flexibility in his artistic responses and in his ability at composition. Even the practical end of teaching writing is not met, if a student writer is not aware that the same words cannot appear in a book, a public speech, a television programme, a radio programme, and a drama. The study of form and structure would enable the student to develop adaptability to these kinds of situations.

It is imperative that anything learned in the complex world of today be learned in such a way as to permit transference. The transfer value of the humanities has always been their greatest strength and, in fact, has been the keystone of the liberally educated man, whether the aristocratic courtier of the Renaissance or the gentleman of taste in the eighteenth century. To rediscover the ways to make English language and literature the core of all learning, which it has been and should be, requires a major revision of this area of study.

REPORT OF THE

Social Sciences Study Committee

C. B. MACPHERSON (CHAIRMAN)

EVAN CRUIKSHANK

LLOYD DENNIS

WM. SAGER

JOHN SAYWELL

NOTE. *Professor Harold Nelson, an original member of the Committee, was not able to take part in the Committee's work after the spring of 1961, but wishes to associate himself with the main objectives and recommendations of the report.*

1. PRELIMINARIES

Members of the Social Sciences Study Committee have examined the content and teaching of the courses in Social Studies, History, and Geography, from Grades 1 to 13. We have, throughout, had in mind the needs of those students who do not go on to university, as well as of those who do. This raised no problem, for we found that the criteria of adequacy in these subjects were the same for both groups: what is good for one group is good for the other.

We came fairly quickly to the conclusion that fundamental improvement was to be sought not in drawing up an ideal sequence of courses in terms of content, but in attempting changes in the way the content is handled. However, we were forced back to some recommendations about content. For although the way the content is handled, and the purposes for which it is taught, do ultimately depend on the quality of the teachers, they also depend partly on the prescription of content and on the text-books. The best teacher is wasted on an empty course, or on a cluttered course; either also encourages the indifferent teacher's indifference.

Our general position therefore has been to take the present sequence of courses as an acceptable framework, and only to recommend changes in content, or in sequence of content, where such changes are required to bring within reach of attainment the objectives which we believe desirable. We find that neither our objectives nor the objectives officially set out by the Ontario Department of Education are now within reach of achievement by any but the most exceptional teachers and schools.

Form of the Report

(i) The order of presentation of our findings will be different from the order of discovery. The committee, and individual members of it, have worked their way backwards and forwards many times between practice and objectives, between statements of aims and analysis of the actual situation (courses, examinations, text-books, classroom teaching). We have emerged with a critical reconsideration of the objectives of teaching these subjects in the schools; an analysis of the present practice, and of the sources of its deficiencies (measured either by the official Departmental objectives or by our own restatement of objectives); and some proposals for overcoming the deficiencies. Although we present our views in this order, we hope it will not be thought that we moved only from abstract to concrete.

(ii) While no amount of evidence in matters of this sort can produce absolutely valid conclusions, the weight of evidence that seemed to be needed for different parts of our analysis varied. We have generally found that the evidence available to us was sufficient to allow us to make proposals with some confidence; we have equally generally found that continuing study would be advantageous, and we have made some specific recommendations to that effect.

(iii) We have found also that to make our analysis, whether of objectives or of practice, at all useful, we have had for the most part to deal separately with different groups of grades. Although it was possible to say something about over-all objectives, the objectives and problems change a good deal between Grade 1 and Grade 13. The most convenient divisions appeared to be Grades 1 to 4, Grades 5 to 8, Grades 9 to 13.

(iv) We had to decide whether, in the secondary school grades at least, history and geography were of such different character that they needed to be discussed separately. Geography, as it is now treated by its specialist teachers and by the Department, is a study whose roots are substantially, though not entirely, in some of the natural sciences. To the extent that geography is built on these natural science foundations, the objectives and the problems of teaching and learning in geography are different from the objectives and problems of teaching and learning in history. In both subjects, students should be brought to see how generalizations are reached from observed and recorded fact. Both deal, in part, with the way men are related to their physical environment. But to the extent that geography is treated as a natural science, the emphasis in its teaching must be on ensuring that the scientific concepts, facts, and laws, are grasped correctly. In a natural science, correctness is an essential. In history it is not: if history is treated as a series of correct facts, or a series of correct relations between facts, it would be better not taught at all. However, the difference between history and the kind of geography now officially recognized in the schools is not as great as the difference between history and a natural science. Geography stands, in method and aims, somewhere between history and natural science: it uses some of the methods, and some of the data, of both, for it is concerned with the relation of man to his environment. It does not claim for its generalizations the degree of certainty usually claimed for scientific laws; in this respect it is nearer to history than to the natural sciences. We found, then, that history and geography did not have to be treated entirely separately. The present deficiencies, and the changes needed to overcome them, are much the same in both subjects.

(v) Our report therefore takes the following form. After some brief comment on the general design of the Ontario curricula in Social Studies, History, and Geography (section 2), and a critical restatement of objectives (section 3), we turn to the problems of each of the three groups of grades: Grades 1 to 4 Social Studies (section 4), Grades 5 to 8 Social Studies and History and Geography (section 5), Grades 9 to 13 History and Geography (section 6). In each of these sections we confront practice with objectives, analyse the shortcomings of practice, and propose remedies.

2. THE GENERAL DESIGN OF THE ONTARIO CURRICULUM

Sequence of Courses

The Committee appreciates the purpose of, and has not proposed any alteration in, the general design of the sequence of courses in the social science subjects. The general design seeks to ensure some measure of completeness for those who will leave school at the end of Grade 10, at the end of Grade 12, and at the end of Grade 13, and it tries, within that framework, to provide a gradually widening and deepening understanding of the subject-matter.

We do not suppose that the present sequence of courses is perfect. At some points it is clearly imperfect, as where a newly instituted course of study for some one or two grades does not exactly adjust to or overlaps with the unchanged adjacent grades. Instances of this will be mentioned specifically. We shall argue also that the sequence of courses, as it now stands, has produced faults in the substance of certain courses: it has led to the material being spread too thin in some grades and crowded too thick in others. These faults, the results of previous changes in the sequence, can be remedied by two or three further changes, and we make specific recommendations about this.

While the present faults of repetition, thinness, and clutter, are important enough to merit action, there are more serious faults which cannot be remedied by mere revision of the sequence of courses, though remedy does involve some revision of the content of many of the courses. The case for more fundamental changes is made in the main body of the report. But something may be said here about the methods of curricular revision, for they have a bearing on piecemeal changes as well as on the more fundamental changes.

Methods of Curricular Revision

It is apparent that changes in the curriculum are continuing, and will continue, to be made by the Department. We are aware of the difficulties of curricular revision. But we doubt that it can satisfactorily be done by the present method, which too often consists of slow deliberation by Departmental officials interspersed with sudden and hurried consultations of an *ad hoc* group of active teachers. A new curriculum for one or two grades cannot decently be drafted in three or four Saturdays by any group of teachers.

There is a serious problem here. It is clear that the decisions on curriculum must be made by the Department, however much leeway it may allow to local Boards and teachers for interpretation and experiment. Yet the Departmental officials, though former teachers, are necessarily remote from teaching and from professional knowledge of the subject-matter of the various disciplines. They can, and do, call on teachers and university professors to advise them on particular changes, but the consultation even on piecemeal changes is frequently too little and too late.

The necessary remoteness of Departmental officials from academic knowledge of the subjects has a more serious consequence: changes initiated by the Department are apt to be confined to changes in the sequence of courses or in the prescription of the factual content of courses. The Department has indeed recognized the inadequacy of such changes, and has gone some way to meet it by giving local Boards and teachers some freedom of interpretation and some room for experiment. But it appears to us that some more effective continuous consultative procedures should now be devised, encouraging more continuous initiative from below.

Continuous Learning

The Committee has not been impressed by the view that there should be continuous building of knowledge and understanding from Grade 1 to the Ph.D., with never a fresh start and never any unlearning. There is of course a strong case for not wasting the energies of students and teachers, at any level, on work which has to be unlearned at the next higher level. We use this principle ourselves in some of our recommendations (e.g., in section 4). But it should not be expected that nothing should ever have to be unlearned. The degree of understanding of society which can be expected of, or which it would be at all possible to try to provide for, a student who leaves school at the end of Grade 10, is (to take an extreme example) so different from what can be expected of and provided for a student in the later years at university, that the latter student may well have to unlearn something somewhere in between. Unlearning something is merely recognizing that the explanation that was accepted as satisfactory at the earlier level is not satisfactory at the more advanced level. The earlier knowledge must be dropped not because it is false (for it is not absolutely false) but because it is at the more advanced level relatively false, and therefore inadequate. Newton is superseded by Einstein, but Newton is still useful. There is in our view no cause for alarm if, at some of the upper levels, students have to start again and reject what they knew in any subject. But there is cause for alarm if they have been so taught at any level that they regard the necessity of starting again, when they meet it, as an evil, or so taught that they are incapable of starting again.

3. OBJECTIVES OF HISTORY, GEOGRAPHY, AND SOCIAL STUDIES AS SCHOOL SUBJECTS

General statements, official and otherwise, of the desirable objectives in the teaching of history and geography are easy to come by. All the ones we have seen are very nice. If some of them have an air of unreality it is perhaps because their authors have begun by taking it for granted that history and geography are subjects that will always be in the curriculum, and have then projected onto them such of the generally desirable educational goals as the subject-matter seemed best able to bear.

It will be better to begin by asking what if anything would be lost if history and geography, as presently prescribed and taught, were dropped entirely, and the time now given to them were given to other subjects. How much if anything would be lost depends on the larger question as to what we want schooling as a whole to do. Apart from the school's broadest and most indispensable social functions of protecting the child against exploitation and protecting society against the child, which functions are performed no matter what the curriculum, its essential task is to prepare the future adult to live in less than complete confusion in an increasingly complex society, in which the rate of change is changing, not only in science and technology, but in human relationships of all kinds—familial, political, economic, and social.

The most hopeful antidotes to confusion are an ability to communicate and be communicated with. This requires an ability to read and to speak or write clearly, at least to frame clear sentences and combinations of sentences; an ability to distinguish between what is relevant and irrelevant to a given decision, and to distinguish between normative and factual statements; and an acquaintance with the concepts of at least Western culture, within and by means of which an individual's thinking, decisions, and communication must be carried on. Without these, a student is not likely to understand the subjects he studies in school, let alone cope with the world when he gets out into it. To the ability to communicate, defined thus broadly, might be added an ability to think mathematically or scientifically, at least to the point where a student is able to understand a little of the quantitative basis of modern science and technology.

These may seem modest as minimum goals of schooling: when we consider how far short of them our present system falls we might rather set them up as maximum goals. They are obviously goals for mass education, but they are also prerequisites of higher education. In the measure that they can be attained they should reduce both the waste of resources in higher education, and the bewilderment and dupery (moral, political, and commercial) which are so stultifying and so dangerous in our contemporary culture.

What, then, in respect of these goals, would be lost if there were no formal subjects called history, geography, or social studies, in our schools? We may leave out of account here the goal of acquaintance with quantitative reasoning. The social studies, at school level, do not and are not expected to contribute to this in any significant degree; this is a task for school mathematics and science. It is in respect of the first broad goal— the ability to communicate and be communicated with, clearly and critically, which includes an acquaintance with the concepts of our culture —that history and geography may be expected to be relevant.

When the question of relevance is faced, the case for history and geography, or social studies, is bleak. It is not at all self-evident that much would necessarily be lost. Surprisingly, in view of the longer-established prestige of history as a school subject, at least in the later grades, it is geography that seems most secure by this test. Something indeed would be lost if there were no geography at all, under whatever name. Future citizens should know where places are; for this, a minimum of the old-style geography is indispensable. The more scientific kind of geography that has recently been brought into the schools is another matter. Part of the new geography is simply natural science: rock formations, air currents, climate, and so on: this much could be put into the natural sciences curriculum. The other part of the new geography deals with the ways in which the natural environment, scientifically described, determines society and culture. Some grasp of this, at however elementary a level, may be thought indispensable to any understanding of culture and society. It is difficult to see how it could be taught as anything except geography or social studies. Yet the full curriculum in geography goes beyond what is indispensable. The new geography seeks not merely to say where places are, what are their physical features, what are their natural resources, their products, and their exports. It seeks to develop an intellectual discipline investigating the necessary and possible relations between man, society, the economy, and the diverse natural environments of the world. Geography so conceived can, if well taught, be a stimulating and illuminating intellectual activity: it is meritorious though not indispensable. But too often it is not so taught. Official recognition of geography's claim to be an intellectual discipline in its own right has won it a larger place in the curriculum, but the larger place is often filled merely by a greater quantity of descriptive material. No one would consider such learning indispensable.

The claims of history are older, and are in all the more need of being looked at. It is clear that history as it might be taught is capable of acquainting students with at least Western culture. And it is arguable that history might be so taught in schools as to contribute to a student's ability to distinguish between normative and factual propositions. But it is not clear that history as a school subject is indispensable for either of these purposes. Could not the students' introduction to their own culture and society, and to that of others, and even to their change over time, be as well or better provided by an expanded course in literatures? And could not the ability to distinguish between relevant and irrelevant, and between normative and factual, be better acquired by formal study of logic and rhetoric (whatever one might now prefer to call them)?

The committee does not press these questions. We have some regard for the limits of practicable reform, and if these questions were to be answered in the affirmative the curriculum reform that would be implied would no doubt be politically impracticable. But it is worth asking occasionally if the emperor has any clothes, while avoiding the juvenile error of asserting that he has none.

We are saying that history and geography are not entirely indispensable, and that both, as now taught, are not automatically to be assumed to be the most efficient instruments for achieving the broad goals outlined. They may be. But the case has to be made. History and geography might be so taught that the case would be proven. But it is our impression, confirmed by the kind of examinations set in all grades, that apart from a small percentage of unusually imaginative teachers, history and geography are not so taught. And we are clear that history and geography cannot be so taught by the average teacher when, as now, he is encouraged or required to cover a stated amount of ground (whether it be all or less than all the contents of the prescribed text-book) and that ground is of such extent that, in order to grind the facts in to the student, neither he nor the student can think much about the selection of facts, the evidence for the facts, or the problem of interpreting and relating the facts.

No one denies that facts are necessary in history. But too few realize that facts are secondary. The same may be said about the new geography. Facts are only instrumental to the purposes of history, only instrumental to the purposes proposed here, or to those proposed in the official statements of the Department. The official statements of the Department (e.g., Curriculum S.9, Senior Division History, 1959, p. 4, para. 4) recognize this, but the quantity of factual information that is then prescribed to be "covered" appears to us effectively to deny it. History is treated as a body of knowledge that must be acquired by anybody who is to become a good citizen; the amount of it that can be taught in one grade up to a creditable examination level is taken as given (properly enough, since, given the type of factual examination, the amount of material it is feasible to cover can fairly easily be determined by experience or experiment); and the problem of curriculum prescription for that grade then becomes simply a matter of seeing how many chunks of history that somebody thinks important can be got in, or how few can be left out. When a curriculum is changed, it is changed by regretfully leaving out the Palace of Cnossus in order to put in the story of the United Nations (Curriculum S.9, p. 4).

This betrays a concept of the role of school history which we think seriously defective. The reasoning seems to be that since the problems of the world are becoming increasingly complex it is urgent to get more information about modern events into the curriculum. Given this reasoning, the pressure to get more and more facts into the curriculum is continuous and intense, so that the quantity of information prescribed is maintained at a level that can easily, and in our view does in fact, generally preclude any of it being understood. The danger has been recognized by the Department. Official recognition of the danger has, in the case of Grade 12, led to the tragi-comical expedient of setting out a table showing which pages of each of the authorized texts are to be mastered in detail and "prescribed for examinations," which pages are to be merely "read and discussed in the classroom," and which are "for extensive treatment . . . not prescribed for note-making or examinations" (Curriculum S.9, pp. 26–29).

The problems of the world are indeed becoming increasingly complex, but it does not follow that it is urgent to get more information about modern events into the curriculum. What does follow, if we are thinking of producing responsible democratic citizens, is that students should be able to read newspapers and news magazines, and perhaps even books, sceptically, and with some notion of the value of evidence, some notion of relevance and irrelevance, and some discrimination between facts and prejudices (other people's prejudices at least, and perhaps even their own). They should also be able to talk about the news (we use the word "news" to mean all the information and editorializing provided in the press and on the air about the problems of the modern world), with the same notions of relevance, evidence, and discrimination between fact and opinion; without some ability of this sort, they cannot pull their weight in the democratic process. If we are thinking about preparing students for university, the same objectives are the important ones: the only difference is that such students should certainly be able to read books, and should be able to discuss all topics more precisely.

None of these urgent objectives can be reached by filling a student's mind, or burdening his retentive capacity, with a rapidly covered lot of information about the United Nations or the events of the last ten or fifty years in Germany, or about the history of Europe or England or Canada or Rome in the nineteenth or seventeenth or first century. The "modern" information will be forgotten or out-of-date by the time the student turned citizen needs to use it; the rest will be forgotten at the end of each school year.

If a student does not get from his school work in history the critical abilities here emphasized, virtually the whole of the time he has spent studying history is an appalling waste. All he will have is a slight cultural deposit, useful in quiz games and valuable to the tourist industry. Virtually the same may be said about his work in geography.

4. SOCIAL STUDIES, GRADES 1–4

Stated Purposes Examined

The persons responsible for the Ontario *Programme of Studies for Grades* 1–6, and for the Toronto Board's Outlines Grades 1–8, have exercised notable intelligence and ingenuity in fulfilling the directive of the

Ontario Department that courses in Social Studies must be produced for all these grades. The strain was clearly greatest in the earlier grades. They have filled up the space and time, and done so in accordance with the two general directives which can be inferred from the statement "Purpose of the Social Studies" (Ontario *Programme of Studies for Grades* 1–6, p. 65) i.e., "to help the child to understand the nature and working of the social world in which he lives," and "to develop in the pupils desirable social attitudes."

No one can quarrel with the first purpose: it is precisely right. The second purpose is debatable at two levels: first, as to whether the inculcation of social attitudes should be a purpose of institutional education at all; and second, as to whether it should be a function allotted especially to Social Studies.

The committee does not propose to debate the first of these questions. The use of the schools for moral acculturation seems to be firmly established, and is probably inevitable at least in our urban society. Granting, then, that it is a necessary function of the school in the earliest grades to try to inculcate desirable social attitudes and principles of behaviour, there is still the question whether this should be attempted in Social Studies specifically.

The desirable social attitudes are given as "consideration for others, willingness to accept responsibility and to work with others in order to get things done; attitudes of helpfulness and loyalty to friends, home, school, and community" (Ontario *Programme*, p. 65). Much the same purposes are set out earlier in the *Programme* (p. 6) with reference to the task of the school as a whole:

Members of such a society need to know how to help one another to get things done. Educators accordingly attach great importance to the development and exercise of those qualities that enable the individual "to work with other people," "to get along with others," "to act in a socially acceptable manner," "to develop a socially satisfactory personality," "to be a good citizen." Co-operation in a democratic group requires self-control, intelligent self-direction, and the ability to accept responsibility.*

It is then pointed out that these qualities, or "the habit of effective behaviour in accord with the principles of democratic living," cannot be "acquired from the verbal teaching of precept" but "can be learned only through meaningful social experience at the child's own age level." This

---

*One wonders what force the quotation marks are intended to have. They seem to be there as an apology for the tiredness of the phrases. Should the concept, as well as the phrases, be retired?

must presumably cut across all courses of study in each grade. The meaningful social experience must come through relationships between teacher and pupil, and between pupil and pupil, which cannot be confined to one subject.

It has clearly been assumed, however, by those who have drawn up the curriculum, that the subject of social studies is peculiarly suited to developing the desired social attitudes and behaviour. It has been assumed that in social studies one can without danger move into "verbal teaching of precepts," because in social studies, as in no other subject of the primary grades, precepts can be made to seem to grow out of the elementary factual concepts. It is in social studies that the first elementary concept of the social division of labour and the consequent actual and necessary interdependence of individuals, in the family and in the local and wider community, is properly introduced. What is more natural, then, than to move directly from that to the precept that each individual should be co-operative, helpful, and tolerant? There thus seems to be a happy marriage between the two stated aims of the social studies course—"to help the child to understand the nature and working of the social world in which he lives" and "to develop in the pupils desirable social attitudes."

We doubt if it is a happy marriage. There is reason to think that it is a forced and unhappy one. We shall not enter into the philosophical question whether it is proper to deduce moral precepts from factual propositions. We grant that it is proper to do so. But it is not proper to confuse the two, to make them seem as if they were all one.

To confuse the actual with the desirable, to confuse the proposition that all individuals are dependent on each other with the injunction that we should all be helpful to each other, is not only improper but harmful in its later effects. Yet the confusion repeatedly occurs, even in the most carefully prepared outlines: it is almost unavoidable, given the confusion in the original curricular assumptions. Thus we find, among the "Lesson Concepts" in the Toronto Board's Outline for Grade 1, "Mother does not waste food or time" (p. I–1), "Father cares for his property" (p. I–2), "Policemen are always ready and willing to help people in trouble" (p. III–4), "Parents help each other by doing those things most suitable to each other" (p. III–5), "The teacher is the friend of *every* child in the class" (p. V–2), etc. Such moral precepts presented as factual propositions are mixed indiscriminately with properly factual propositions and (a few) properly moral injunctions.

Confusion of the actual with the desirable seems to go very deep in the curricula of the primary grades. It is not, in our opinion, simply a matter of methodological slips, which could easily be remedied. It seems to reflect a desire to protect the children from harsher realities. Since the children have to be assimilated to society, and since it is thought desirable to do this by providing a rationale rather than by coercion, the curriculum-makers put the best moral face they can on society and present it as fact.

The harm this may do, the impediment it may be to later real learning, can best be considered after a closer look at the content of the material offered for the teachers' use.

Damaging Effect of the Purposes

The social universe of family, neighbourhood, community, and economic society which is presented in Grades 1 and 2 is all neat, pleasant, helpful, and suburban. It is wholly false in some of the pupils' experience, partly false in others', and can be wholly true in almost none (for even those who do live in such a pleasant physical environment rarely live in such model social relationships). The presentation of such a picture of society very nearly negates the avowed purpose of introducing the pupils to the way society operates, at however elementary a level of generalization, and thereby of introducing them to the notion of generalization and generalized concepts (of relationship, etc.) as a way of grasping and understanding a lot of observable phenomena. The wholly laudable design of the social studies in the primary grades—to get a pupil to look theoretically and conceptually at facts which are within his experience, beginning with the family, moving on to the neighbourhood and then to wider communities, and so to develop an understanding of social relations and an ability to think slightly abstractly—is endangered by the falsity of the society presented to him.

Consider the effect of presenting the rosy cosy society as the true model of all social relationships. The child whose family, home, and neighbourhood are not at all clean, neat, and pleasant is being lied to. If he is intelligent he will see this, and will reject school learning as unreal. If he is not intelligent enough to see it clearly, he will be confused and puzzled.

The child whose home, family, and neighbourhood *are* physically like the model is being treated almost as badly. Since the physical part (and perhaps the family relationship part) of the model that is presented to him *does* correspond with his experience, he takes the rest of the model on trust. He has no way of knowing that the helpful and co-operative social and economic relations which are being presented to him as concomitants of the happy comfortable family life are not logically entailed in, and are not actually found everywhere beyond, the comfortable family life he knows. In one sense, this child is being treated far more badly, for he is misled further about the facts beyond his knowledge. Yet he will survive this, and later experience will correct his information.

We are more concerned with the child who sees that the picture is partly wrong and who ends in rejection or confusion. The effect here is serious; this child starts his school life by acquiring an attitude towards learning which is exactly wrong. Later on, in most of his subjects, he will be (or should be) learning how to penetrate through the superficial data of observation to the reality (mathematical, chemical, political, logical, etc.), that is, he will be expected to realize that the world that presents itself to his senses is to some extent an illusion, but that there is a reality behind it which can be grasped. Yet his first introduction to society through these social studies is designed in such a way as to put him off this track. It presents a view of reality behind his own experience which he senses is wrong: he cannot be blamed (but the system can) if his abiding impression (which can go pretty deep at this age) is that there is no use seeking the reality behind the appearance of things.

Content of the Courses

In the general design of the primary curriculum in social studies, the important content is not so much the new information presented to children as the concepts by which they may learn to grasp intellectually what they already know by direct experience. What is required is a balance between conceptualization of information they already have, and acquisition of information (about people, places, and kinds of community and society) which is beyond their direct observation and experience. In our opinion this balance has been achieved in principle in the Toronto Outlines and in some of the text-books.

In Grade 1, the concepts of human interdependence and division of labour are introduced, in the context of the home, the neighbourhood, municipal services, and the school, and the notion of cultural differences is brought in. In Grades 2 and 3 these concepts are further developed and others are introduced: elementary concepts of time, location, distance, and direction; cultural change over time; adaptation to environment as a condition of survival; elementary concepts of prices, wages, rent. Information about ways of life beyond the children's direct experience is fed in: the rural community for urban children, and societies distant in time (Indians) and space (Eskimos) in Canada and beyond Canada. In Grade 4 the social and economic roles of communication and transportation are emphasized and used to show the development of human skills over time; basic information on Canadian industries (extractive, farming, and manufacturing) is given; sketches of the society and geography of a few other countries introduce further information, and provide an opportunity for bringing out the relations between environment and society.

No catalogue of concepts could do justice to the intricacy with which they must be introduced, repeated and developed at the simple levels required in Grades 1 to 4. It is clear that a grasp of these concepts is an essential basis for the later learning process, and we think that the Toronto Outlines have made a valuable contribution in emphasizing them and indicating how they can be handled.

However, we think that the work is stretched unnecessarily thinly in Grades 1 to 3. The present arrangement strongly suggests that it was only the dictates of curricular uniformity (i.e., the decision to have some subject in every grade called Social Studies) that put social studies in Grade 1 at all. Such of the content as is not derisory could quite well enough be given from Grade 2 on. Granted that Grade 1 children can be introduced successfully to the notion of human interdependence and co-operation by being got to think about their family, their neighbourhood, their postman and policeman and school, and granted that they can be introduced successfully to these notions only at the very rudimentary level implicit in the present Grade 1 Outline, it nevertheless appears to us that introduction to these notions could well be left until Grade 2, where in any case it is all done again in relation to the local community. This would spare pupil and teacher the present unavoidable fatuity of lessons about "mother's work," "father goes to work," and the egregious redundancy of a teacher teaching a lesson about a teacher. If Grade 1 social studies were dropped entirely, an hour a day for a year would be saved, which could we presume be well used in English or some other subjects. Whatever is of value in the Grade 1 course could be merged into the Grade 2 course, with which it overlaps a great deal now. The abolition of Grade 1 social studies might have an additional advantage. If it is assumed that children arriving in Grade 1 are anxious to learn something they didn't already know, their interest is more likely to be sustained if they can see that they are learning something new. They are more likely to see this in their achievements in reading and writing or indeed in almost any other subject than social studies as arranged at present in Grade 1. For while they are (or should be) in fact learning something from the present Grade 1 social studies, what they are learning is something so abstract (namely, the ability to think in rudimentary generalizations) that they cannot see they are learning anything. All they *see* is pap—mother works at home, the postman brings the mail—which is not news to them. It is not very conducive to a child's appreciation of learning. Moreover, since the material in the Grade 1 course is so thin, a teacher is encouraged to fill it up with moralizing, which again is not very conducive to a child's appreciation of learning.

It appears to us that the case for taking social studies out of Grade 1 entirely is a strong one, on the assumption that Grade 1 children are not capable of being introduced to rudimentary social concepts at a level higher than that implied in the present Grade 1 Outline. However, if it were assumed (or if it were found by experiment) that Grade 1 children could take the present Grade 2 work in their stride, it might be desirable to move the content for 2, 3, and 4 down to 1, 2, and 3, and fill up the year at Grade 4 with, say, some more solid work in geography than is at present attempted. Or something more solid might be added to the old Grades 3 and 4, so that there would then be a new and expanded 2, 3, and 4. There would be an endless range of possibilities, but choice among them would have to depend on experimental classes.

It would be simpler and probably more satisfactory simply to take social studies out of Grade 1, and merge it with the present Grade 2 work.

A case could be made, on the same grounds as the case for taking social studies out of Grade 1, for taking them out of Grade 2 as well, and covering all that is now spread over Grades 1 to 4 in Grades 3 and 4, releasing the time in Grade 2 as well as that in Grade 1 for work in other subjects. The net gain or loss of doing so would have to be established by experiment. There is considerable overlapping now between Grades 2 and 3 —both start with house-building, both deal with shopping in the local stores, etc. The questions are whether anything like the present amount of repetition is needed to develop the elementary concepts of interdependence etc. which run through the whole of Grades 1 to 3; whether the repetition does more good (in getting the concepts established gradually and firmly) than harm (in trivializing, and dulling the appetite for learning); and, if more good than harm, whether as much good could not be done by devoting the time to other subjects.

It may be objected that to remove social studies from Grade 1 and to reduce even further the time given to it over Grades 1 to 4, would remove a substantial part of the present "natural" opportunity of inculcating desirable social attitudes. We have already stated our grounds for believing that social studies should not be treated as such a natural opportunity, and that at the earliest grades more harm than good (as measured by a child's later attitude towards *learning*) is likely to result from the attempt. We have, however, recognized that the inculcation of social attitudes by the school is unavoidable. It may therefore still be objected that the process should begin in Grade 1, and that something like the present Grade 1 lessons are necessary for it. Granting that the process should begin in Grade 1, we are not convinced that the present Grade 1 lessons are indeed necessary. The attitudes which the present Grade 1 lessons are designed to inculcate comprise some which are so general (acceptance of authority, helpfulness to others, tolerance towards other ways, respect and appreciation of new Canadians) that they can and should come from the example of the teacher and the activities of the classroom in all subjects, and some which are so particular (don't waste bread, address letters correctly, look out for the traffic) as not to require to be dressed up as Social Studies. All of them together scarcely require 20 per cent of a child's time (an hour a day for the 197 days of the school year).

Summary of Recommendations, Grades 1 *to* 4

(i) That social studies be removed from Grade 1 and the time devoted to other subjects.

(ii) That experimental classes be used to assess the net gain or loss from reducing by about one-third the amount of time given to the present social studies work in Grades 2 to 4, and devoting this time to more solid work in geography or to work in some of the other subjects.

(iii) Alternatively to (i) and (ii), that experimental classes be used to assess the net gain or loss of moving the present Grade 2 social studies work into Grade 1 and introducing in Grades 2 to 4 more solid learning, chiefly geographical, alongside most of the present Grade 3 and 4 work.

(iv) That outlines of courses, and text-books, abandon the rosy cosy view.

(v) That outlines of courses, and text-books, avoid confusing moral precepts and factual generalizations.

5. GRADES 5–8

Grades 5 to 8 make up a critical period. The student after these four years of study should be sufficiently trained to face the demands that high-school history and geography should make. These years are critical not only in terms of training, but also in terms of interest. Four unhappy years with social studies at this point can effectively kill any interest in the subject for the rest of a student's life.

Grade 5: Content and Treatment

Since this is the first true history or social science course a student confronts, it is essential that some beginning be made in familiarizing him with the basic concepts, skills, and mental attitudes that will henceforth be needed in this area of study.

As stated by the Department, the theme of the course is "rolling back the clouds" and its aim is to "reveal the world to the child as it was revealed to the discoverers and explorers." "From the stories of these men," the Department hopefully suggests, should emerge a "wide acquaintance with the earth's geography" and, to summarize, some elementary anthropology. The objectives listed for each unit in the Toronto Board's Outline are less ambitious and more specific, but seem generally to be based on what might be extracted from each unit of the courses in the Departmental curriculum, rather than on what might be accomplished given the time and subject-matter. The Outline, in other words, has some of the critical weaknesses of the course as devised and outlined by the Department and does not offer any new approach to the Grade 5 course

It may be said, incidentally, that the Outline adds to the weakness by its use of the word "concept." What are set out as "Lesson Concepts" (in all the Outlines from Grades 1 to 8) are for the most part not concepts at all but summary statements of facts ("Commodities of civilized Europe aided the explorers in trade relations with natives they encountered"), statements of single facts ("Magellan's voyage was sponsored by Spain"), generalizations from facts ("Different waters of the world present different problems to navigation"), and even simply listings of specific things to be included in the lessons ("Basic Geography of Australia," "Climate of Region"). To lump these together as "Concepts" is perhaps not as harmful as the confusion of moral and factual propositions we remarked in the earlier grades (which is also done under the heading "Lesson Concepts"), but it can be disturbing for a teacher. By extinguishing the difference between facts and abstraction the Outline is derogatory about abstraction, and thus weakens its general design of leading a child from fact to abstraction or conceptualization. "Lesson Concepts" might better be called something else.

We agree that the subject-matter of the Grade 5 course is excellent for the grade level. The story approach is unquestionably essential. Yet while this approach must be retained it is equally essential that the stories be fitted into some pattern. At most, they should be treated as the coating of sugar which makes the objectives of the course palatable, though this is perhaps an insult to the desire of students of that age to learn something.

While the determination of the exact timing of the introduction of concepts or general principles would demand an experimental research programme beyond the scope of this committee, we have assumed that three ideas should be systematically introduced here: the idea of chronology; causation of an immediate nature; and causation that may be described as removed from the actual events themselves.

If this be admitted, the present course is at once open to severe criticism. Neither as outlined, nor as written in the approved texts, nor as taught in the majority of the classrooms, are these principles effectively introduced. Indeed, in leaving the students with the impression that explorers explored because they were explorers, the course may retard genuine historical learning or thinking. The essential question in all the social sciences, WHY, is not, as it should be, made the constant focus.

We may give one illustration. In all probability, more time is spent on Captain Cook than on any other single person in the Grade 5 course. The following conversation took place between a committee member and a student of well above average ability.

"Who was Cook?"	"An explorer."
"Where did he explore?"	"The Pacific."
"Why?"	"Because he was an explorer."
"What nationality was he?"	No answer, although after running through a number of nationalities the student concluded that he might have been English.
"Why was he sent?"	"Because he was an explorer"— presumably unemployed.
"Had he ever done anything significant?"	Pause. Finally, "He fought with Wolfe at Quebec."
"Who was Wolfe?"	No answer.
"When?"	No answer.
"Why Quebec?"	No answer.

Yet this student could rehearse the details of Cook's three voyages and could, one imagines, have done a first-class map. But all the essential questions: why the British were concerned about the Pacific; what prompted them to begin Pacific exploration; the power struggle in the Pacific (and in western Europe); the importance of sea routes and prevailing winds; the changing nature of English society and economy—in short, all the questions that make Cook make sense—were never asked or answered.

The same could be said of most other sections in the course. The Portuguese reach India. Europeans from small countries meet Asians from big ones. What happened then? How was the West able to impose its control of the rest of the word? And with what results? None of these questions, in however elementary a way, is introduced. Moreover, the world appears to have been opened by people as pleasant as the friendly postman in the elementary grades. This is unreal, even unintentionally dishonest; the damage, pointed out earlier, of presenting an unreal picture of society, is compounded.

The committee's recommendations for getting full value from this course may now be stated. They are stated at some length, as most of them apply to the later grades of public school as well as to Grade 5.

Recommendations for Grade 5, mainly applicable also to Grades 6–8

(i) That the emphasis of the present Grade 5 course be changed so as to make the narrative approach (which should be kept) lead to some notion of historical and geographical causal patterns.

(ii) That, to implement (i), a manual of say 150 pages be prepared, which would give teachers the history and geography they need to know in order to teach what they ought to teach in Grade 5 social studies. Such a manual, by showing them the problems and questions involved in the material, would at the same time help them with handling the material in class. (Similar manuals should be prepared for Grades 6 to 8 also.)

(iii) That an extensive programme of in-service training, differing in two respects from the in-service training now available, be developed. (*a*) It should be training in the subject, rather than in the technique of teaching. The average Grade 5 teacher will need some assistance before she can make any sense of the expansion of Europe which, in effect, is what this course is about. What is needed is opportunity and encouragement for the teacher to think about the subject. (*b*) It should be more extensive than the present in-service training. Four late afternoons a term, with no time off from teaching, and no monetary inducement, are not good enough. Such training needs time off, and salary inducements.

(iv) That to implement (iii), the number of social studies consultants be increased.

Any or all of these four steps could be taken by a local Board. They do not depend on, although they could be rendered more effective by, changes at the level of the Ontario Department.

The committee recognizes, however, that these steps could not by themselves remedy the present situation. At most, they would repair, for some of the teachers, some of the defects of the Teachers' College training which now qualifies them for employment as teachers. The present training is designed to produce people who can handle public school classes, not people who can handle subjects. When the needs of the province as a whole are considered, needs ranging from those of small rural schools to those of large urban schools, the necessity of training such teachers is clear. The trend towards consolidated rural schools is doing something to alter this necessity throughout the province. But it has already been altered beyond recognition in large urban areas, by the development of senior public schools and of the system of rotating classes among subject teachers. In such urban areas it has now become possible to use teachers who, over and above their general training in handling classes, have been trained specifically for teaching certain subjects. We therefore further recommend:

(v) That the Teachers' College course be reorganized to give some part of the time to training in subjects. The question immediately arises whether this is possible within the present one-year training course. We are of the opinion that it should be tried. A student teacher would have to choose, sometime in the first term, which division (primary, junior, or intermediate) he or she wanted to be trained for, and, if junior or intermediate, which subjects. He could then, from January on, devote, say, two hours a day to the special subject, for example, Junior Division Social Studies, or Intermediate Division History.

This would be better than nothing. But more would be better. In view of the fact that the Department now provides an extra year of training for one category of teachers who are recognized to need special skills, namely Kindergarten teachers, there is a case for an extra year of training at the Teachers' Colleges, in subject-matter, for those who choose to teach intermediate and junior divisions. We do not press this case, but we recommend:

(vi) That serious consideration be given to the early introduction of a two-year Teachers' College course.

Since, as we noticed earlier, the need for the changes recommended in either (v) or (vi) above, is not likely to be felt as strongly on a province-wide scale as in the urban areas whose Boards could take full advantage of it, we recommend:

(vii) That the Toronto Board, perhaps with other large urban area Boards, should explore with the Ontario Department the possibility of setting up under joint auspices a Teachers' College, or a special course within some existing Teachers' Colleges, to provide the sort of training, in Social Studies, History, and Geography, recommended in (v) or (vi).

(viii) To implement (v) or (vi), urban Boards who can use teachers trained in subjects would have to be prepared to seek and appoint specialists for at least Grades 7 and 8, as they now do for the secondary grades.

As noted earlier, our consideration of the problems of Grade 5 Social Studies has led us into a series of recommendations of which all but the first apply as much (or more) to Grades 6 to 8 as to Grade 5. In going on now to the problems of Grades 6, 7, and 8 we confine ourselves to matters requiring additional specific attention.

Grade 6: Content and Recommendation

The Grade 6 course in North American exploration is clearly a logical follow-up from Grade 5. It is equally clearly an absurdity in view of the new Grade 7 course, where the students once again paddle their way across and around the continent. Although the Departmental instructions refer to this overlapping and warn the Grade 7 teacher that exploration should be taken as known, we can safely assume that the instructions are generally ignored. The texts in Grade 7 bear this out.

Unless we are to conclude that exploration is worth the better part of two years (in which case it will effectively destroy a student's interest in Canadian history) the question must be raised: where should it be taught? The committee feels that the answer is obvious. It must be taught in Grade 7, for otherwise Canadian history before 1800 makes no sense at all.

We risk this generalization in the belief that exploration for its own sake is not important, whatever the present Grade 6 course may assume. (The course has most of the weaknesses of the Grade 5 course, already discussed.) The exploration of North America, for both geography and history students, only makes sense when it is placed in the meaningful pattern of continental economic and political rivalry and related to the socio-economic structure, the geographical factors, and the political dynamism of the community that spawns the explorers. The committee therefore recommends:

(i) That the present Grade 6 course be removed from the curriculum.

Suggested Alternatives, Grades 5–8

Any revision of the programme for Grades 5 to 8 consequent on the removal of the present Grade 6 course would demand a fairly extensive study. The following possibilities are worth considering:

(i) Grade 5: The Ancient World—an elementary course of the social studies kind, introducing the student to pre-history, the ancient Near Eastern civilizations, and the Graeco-Roman era, with a look at the Middle Ages.

Grade 6 would then take over the present Grade 5 course, as reorganized, and would follow naturally in time and scope.

Grades 7–8: Content left as it is now.

(ii) Leave the present content of Grade 5 where it is, but push that of Grades 7 and 8 back to 6 and 7. Grade 8 could then be advantageously used for (*a*) an introduction to the ancient world, and (*b*) some elementary earth sciences. This progression would lead naturally both into the Grade 9 British history which, in effect, begins with the fall of Rome, and into the regional geography of the eastern hemisphere, which is the substance of Grades 9 and 10 geography. Proposal (ii) would also mean that in Grade 11 history and geography, both very full courses, the teacher might assume some familiarity with the ancient world, and with the elements of systematic geography. It would also have presented a Grade 10 terminal student with a glimmer of the relevance of the contribution of the ancient world to his own.

Grades 7 and 8: History

The Committee found it difficult to assess these courses properly, since they are still in a process of transition. Some teachers are teaching the new history and geography courses, some seem to be attempting a blend of the two, and some seem to be happily ignoring the change completely. Nevertheless, from what has been observed in classrooms, from the Departmental outlines, and from the text-books in print, some observations are possible.

By the end of Grade 8 the students ought to be prepared for what ought to be the demanding work of Grade 9. If the objectives of teaching history at the secondary level are to be met, a student at Grade 9 will be faced with causation—social, economic, and political; with the various types of history; with personal motivation; with institutions and constitutions; with the role of ideas in history; with conflicting interpretations of the past; and with a new and extensive vocabulary. If a student meets all these challenges for the first time the results are apt to be disappointing.

In Grades 7 and 8 the emphasis is still on the narrative, as it should be, but it is narrative at the expense of analysis and explanation. On critical issues, for example, the Seven Years' War, or the American Revolution and Canada's reaction to it, a student does not become involved in the historical process. He is not really made to look at causation; he is not asked to think critically; he is not required to use evidence. A story is told to him and he does his best to remember.

In Grade 8, where only one text is yet available, historical phenomena are subordinated to narrative and to the trivia of social history. The student will fight his way through the war of 1812, but never know how it had come to pass or what it meant. He will clear the land of Upper Canada for weeks, but never be given a chance to understand the rebellions of 1837 or Lord Durham or the whole economic and social break-up in the colonies. "Britain and free trade" gets a bare mention in the fairly full outline (nine pages) in the Departmental Curriculum (I, 1 (c), 1959, p. 17), although it is clearly one of the most momentous events of the century, without which most of what follows does not make sense. It is absurd to expect the student to *understand* what Confederation was all about if he has no real comprehension of the economic structure and orientation of the communities that confederated. (A lack of concern by the Department for explanation is suggested by the placing of Confederation *before* the Civil War. Since the Civil War was a cause of Confederation, surely it should be discussed first.)

The course for the thirty years after Confederation we find badly designed, both from the point of view of history as history and from that of teaching. There appears to be no structure at all: there is no theme, no point, no pattern. The student will dutifully build the railroad and hang Riel, but he will have no idea of why he is doing it and the faculties that will be required in Grade 9 will in no way be developed.

The Committee concludes that history in Grades 7 and 8, as at present handled, will neither prepare students for further work in high school nor inculcate the attitudes and skills whose inculcation justifies the teaching of history in the schools. Intellectually, these courses are neither demanding nor exciting, to say the least.

The whole approach to them needs the same sort of revision, and the revision requires the same sort of improved aids to and training of the teachers, as set out in respect of Grade 5 (recommendations (i) to (viii), above).

Summary of Recommendations, Grades 5 to 8

(i) That the courses now given in Grades 5, 7, and 8 be given in Grades 6, 7, and 8, or 5, 6, and 7, and that the courses, while retaining the narrative approach, be revised to make the narrative lead to some notion of historical and geographical causal patterns. While this re-alignment and revision would fairly soon require different text-books from those now approved, a start could be made, without new books, by taking some of the steps recommended immediately below.

(ii) That manuals be prepared for each of Grades 5 to 8, to give teachers the history and geography they need in order to teach what they ought to teach.

(iii) That in-service training, in subjects rather than in techniques, with more effective incentives and with more time than at present allowed, be provided.

(iv) That the number of social studies consultants be increased.

(v) That the one-year Teachers' College course be revised to give some specialized training in subjects.

(vi) That serious consideration be given to a two-year Teachers' College course.

(vii) That the Toronto Board should explore with the Ontario Department the possibility of Teachers' Colleges courses designed to meet the needs of urban systems which have already developed some subject specialization in their schools.

(viii) That the Toronto Board be prepared to employ specialists in public schools as well as in secondary schools.

(ix) That the present Grade 6 course be removed from the curriculum.

(x) That its place be taken either: (*a*) by moving the present Grade 5 course to Grade 6, and introducing a course in the Ancient World in Grade 5; or (*b*) by moving the present Grades 7 and 8 back to 6 and 7, and putting a course in the Ancient World, and some systematic geography, in Grade 8.

6. HISTORY AND GEOGRAPHY, GRADES 9–13

In this section of the report we deal mainly with the teaching of history, which we were able to analyse more fully than that of geography. We are satisfied, however, that the defects we have found in history are also present already in the more recently established geography. Accordingly, while the analysis is primarily of the teaching of history, we have made our recommendations applicable both to history and to geography.

Sequence of Courses

The sequence of courses in history from Grades 9 to 13 appears to us to be satisfactory, in view of the number of students who leave school at the end of Grade 10 and at the end of Grade 12. British history in Grade 9, and twentieth-century history in Grade 10, should provide some understanding of the modern world for those who leave at the end of 10; ancient and mediaeval history in Grade 11 and modern world history in Grade 12 should deepen the understanding of those who leave at the end of 12; and Canadian-American history is eminently suitable for Grade 13. Some other sequence might be as good or better, but the sequence of subject-matter has no bearing on the real inadequacy of secondary school history, namely, its failure to meet any acceptable objectives, either those set out by the Department or those proposed earlier in this Report.

Contradiction of Objectives

It is difficult to convey in a committee report any sense of the waste of energy and intellectual capacity that now takes place in the learning and teaching of history in the secondary schools. The situation appears to have the elements of classical tragedy: there is no evil intention, it is simply that the forces of institutionalism, which are inevitable, seem necessarily to contradict the very purposes to which society, the educational officials, and those teachers who have not succumbed to routine, themselves subscribe. The victims are (besides the routinized teachers) the students, whose energies are misused, and society, which is not getting what it pays for and what it needs.

We think, however, that this is not a truly tragic situation. The contradiction is not entirely necessary; some remedies may be possible.

What is wrong can be stated very briefly. There is too much grind and not enough thought. That this is true of Grade 13, not only in history but in all subjects, has now, we understand, been officially recognized: the design of Grade 13 as a whole—curriculum and examinations—is now being revised so as to reduce the pressure to cram and increase the possibility of thought. What has not yet apparently been officially recognized is that, in history at least, the same trouble runs through the whole secondary school curriculum.

So much detailed factual material is expected to be "covered" that a teacher has no incentive, but has a strong disincentive, to promote critical discussion, to get the students to read outside the text-book, to confront them with different interpretations of the same events, or to get them to think about fundamental concepts such as power, liberty, and security.

Even those teachers who try merely to cover the curriculum, without much or any attempt to do any of the things just mentioned, rarely (at least in the later secondary grades) succeed in covering it. The exceptional and imaginative teachers who do concentrate on doing these things, do so by leaving large parts of the course untouched. We applaud this expedient, when it is used for purposes of more intelligent teaching. But what more often happens is that large parts are left out in order to drill in the facts in the rest.

Evidence of Inadequacy

The evidence that the whole secondary school curriculum for history suffers from too much fact and not enough thought seems to us to be decisive. It comprises (*a*) the testimony of good secondary school teachers, who are haunted by the waste of young human talent and purpose that is involved in having to prepare students for factual examinations; (*b*) the testimony of university teachers who must spend much of their time trying (often with much less than complete success) to undo what was done to a large proportion of students by the way history was taught them at school; and (*c*) the evidence of examinations including (i) the examinations actually written in 1960 and 1961 in every secondary grade in Toronto schools, (ii) a special examination arranged by the committee in the spring of 1961, and (iii) the experience of the Grade 13 matriculation examinations.

(i) The committee asked for and obtained a complete collection of the history and geography examination papers set in every grade of every secondary school in Toronto, in 1960–61 and/or 1959–60, along with the detailed marking schemes for some of the papers, showing all the points for which marks might be allotted, and a sample of students' answer papers as they had been marked by the teachers in the schools. No clearer documentation of the pre-eminence given to detailed factual information from the text-books could be wanted.

The picture is not all black. Some of the papers show some effort to get beyond mere description. A few contain questions that invite going beyond the text-book. But almost all the papers are heavily weighted towards factual questions to be answered from the information in the text.

Some variation is apparent between the earlier and the later grades. All of the Grade 9 papers demand a lot of detached facts (names, dates, terms of bills and treaties, actions of leading figures). All demand a lot of summaries of connected facts ("describe the three steps taken by . . ."; "how did X bring about policy Y"). Most include a sub-question or two asking for "three causes of" or "two reasons for the importance of" (marks being allotted for material reproduced from a sentence or two of the text). A few include a question asking that specific events be related to a stated trend (e.g., the development of parliamentary government); and a few have a question asking for "an essay" (of two or three paragraphs). But where there is a trend question or an essay question, the time allotted to it is so short as to preclude anything but a summary of points from the text. The overwhelming emphasis of the Grade 9 papers is on purely descriptive material which (the marking schemes show) is expected to be taken from specified pages in the text.

The Grade 10 papers, while still strong on detached facts and pure description, contain rather more questions than found in the Grade 9 papers asking for "significance" or "causes" or asking why something happened, but these are short specific questions, marked by points from the text, and allotted so little time as not to invite thought. The Grade 11 papers seem to revert to the more heavily factual bias of Grade 9. With one notable exception, all the Grade 11 papers ask for less comprehension than the Grade 10 papers. The exception suggests that ancient and mediaeval history, even though more remote than the subject-matter of Grades 9 and 10, need not on that account be treated as series of fixed facts to be learned. The Grade 12 papers in general are up to or beyond the Grade 10 level of demand for causes and significance rather than pure description, but the marking schemes indicate that the marks are still given for points from the text. Papers from two schools go clearly beyond this: one of them asks for an essay of two to three pages, for which 25 per cent of the marks (of a $1\frac{1}{2}$ hour paper) are allotted.

We are aware, of course, that (apart from questions where the marks are explicitly given for identifying names, dates, and places, and other such fragmentary points of fact) it cannot properly be inferred, simply from the wording of a question, whether it does or does not call for more than regurgitation of a part of the text-book or of notes from the blackboard. Whether it does so or not depends on the way it is marked (which the student soon knows). Almost any question, whether it asks the reasons for, the significance of, or the steps leading to, whether it says "Describe" or "Write an essay on," may be asking and giving marks for what was drilled in from the text, or for thought and recollection of past thought. The marking-schemes, and the marked papers, where we have them, leave no doubt that the standard is drilled remembrance, not recollected thought.

But the clearest evidence, even without the marking-schemes and marked answer papers, is in the structure of the question papers. They are almost all chopped up into a number of short questions and sub-questions. As we have said, it is highly exceptional to find a paper that has even one question allotted a quarter of the marks, that is, roughly a quarter of the time (22 minutes). It is much more usual to find questions, which could be answered thoughtfully if there were time, appearing as one of three or four parts of one of four or five questions. It is evident what kind of answer is expected or possible in the 4 to 7 minutes thus allowed. And what are we to say of the question "Discuss fully the rights, responsibilities and problems found in a democratic system" when it is set (as it was on one Grade 12 paper in June 1960) as one of two parts of one of five questions; what could be done with such a question in 9 or 12 minutes?

The prevalent sort of history examination is often defended on the ground that too many students would fail in any other sort. We agree that they would, and that school examinations ought not normally to be such as to fail a high proportion of students. But this defence of the examinations is a condemnation of the teaching. What is at issue here is the kind of teaching that such examinations reflect.

We have no reason to doubt that the fragmentation of knowledge, its reduction to very incompletely comprehended bits of information, which is required or encouraged by the prevalent kind of examinations, accurately reflects the fragmentation in the average classroom, and that this in turn reflects the attempt to "cover" a given amount of the detailed information in the text. What is overlooked is that details were put into the text to show how and why events and institutions took the shape they did, not to be learned as facts in their own right.

(ii) The committee was not content with the evidence of the papers normally set. With the co-operation of some Grade 13 teachers, the committee had a special test paper written in May 1961 by several hundred Grade 13 students. The questions on the paper demanded thought; some of them had no single correct answer or argument. The students were told only that "points" were not the basis for marks. When the answer papers were analysed it was found (1) that many students did try to answer the questions asked; (2) that most students were so inured to the "point" system that, although warned, they knew no other way to answer a question than to grope around for what seemed to them the most relevant pages in the text and give the points from those pages, even though the text material did not quite fit the question; and (3) that there were striking variations in the teaching of different classes. Classes taught by different teachers, who had put different emphases on factual drill, showed a marked difference in ability to bring their minds to bear on problems not answerable directly from remembered textual material; this suggests that the prevalent weaknesses may be surmountable, or at least that they are not inherent in history courses at the secondary school level.

(iii) The experience of the Grade 13 matriculation papers in history is relevant to our problem. It has long been felt that the traditional Grade 13 examinations were inadequate as a testing device for students leaving upper school or entering university. A marking-scheme using the point system tested factual information almost exclusively. The good student could organize his material, select the relevant information, answer the question as asked, and still not get a substantially higher mark, or might even get a lower mark, than the student who filled in three pages with scattered information. The scheme did not permit the examiner to exercise any discretion in appraising the paper on its general merits. The use of presentation marks was an attempt to overcome this deficiency, but this too became so stereotyped that the original purpose was defeated and they became simply a bonus to every student who passed. The only discretion left the examiner was that which is involved merely in measuring an answer, sentence by sentence, against the marking-scheme. The presence of even this amount of subjectivity, it should be said, casts serious doubt on the point system as insurance against widespread variations in marking.

The 1961 history paper introduced a compulsory question which could not be answered satisfactorily simply from a few pages of the text-book. It did not call for much stretch of the candidate's mind, but it did call for a little. It had necessarily to be evaluated not by giving marks for points, but by the markers' subjective appraisal of the candidates' ability to apply information to a question slightly different from any the text would directly have prepared them for. The subjective marking which is required to test anything more than remembrance of points from the text is often said to be impracticable in the circumstances of the matriculation examination. Given the mass of papers, the dozens of markers, the uneven competence of the markers, and the need for uniformity in the interests of the candidates, the case against subjective marking appears formidable. The experience in 1961 does not bear this out. It proved possible, without marking by points, to come as close, if not closer, to fair and uniform marking as can be done by the point system; anyone who has read a few score appeals of papers marked by points knows how erratic the marking by the point system can be.

Would it be feasible, then, to increase the proportion of questions calling for more than points? No doubt the level of ability of markers would have to be improved in order to do justice to such papers. But the problem is not insurmountable. The ability of markers can be expected to adjust itself, with some time-lag, to a change in the nature of the paper, for the change in the paper can be expected to bring out the latent ability not only to teach but to mark more intelligently. Teachers at present, since they must try to get their students successfully through the examinations, must stuff them with points. Perhaps some teachers are, or have become, incapable of any other kind of teaching. But if the precedent of the 1961 history paper is followed, and improved on by increasing the proportion of the paper not calling for points, good teachers will be enabled and indifferent teachers will be induced to teach more intelligently. It is evident that any method of teaching, and examining, works its way down from Grade 13 through all the secondary school grades. We are of the opinion, therefore, that a change in the pattern of the Grade 13 external examination, in the direction begun in 1961, can do a good deal to improve the quality of the teaching and of the product.

We need not take time to argue that drill in facts and memorization of selected* material from a text-book does not meet any defensible

---

*Selected by the teacher, that is. The depths to which the official expectations of student ability have sunk, submerged by the official retention of the "coverage" fetish, is indicated by the Department's instruction to teachers of Grades 11 and 12 history: "To decide . . . what facts are basic and what facts are thrown in for good measure is a first duty of the teacher and a searching test of his scholarship. The pupil is not free to make this decision: he is forced by circumstances to follow in the main the teacher's choice." (Curriculum S.9, 1959, Senior Division History, p. 4.) How searching a test of scholarship it is can be inferred from the fact that the teacher is then referred to the tables on pages 26–29 which offer him a painless selection of pages and parts of pages, of the text-book he is using, suitable for intensive, extensive, and in-between treatment.

objectives of teaching history: this is recognized by all concerned, including the Department. We think we have established that the system now prevailing does not meet any defensible objectives. It does not train the mind; it leaves only a slight cultural deposit in the mind after a few months or a few years; it does not help the student to think abstractly, to look at evidence, or to consider relevance, which we have argued are the main contributions the study of history can be expected to make to the intelligence of the adult and the merit of the citizen.

Nor does such history study help anyone directly to understand the world he must live in. It does not require or induce the student to look behind the particular to the general. He is told indeed that a Reformation or a war had certain causes, but he is rarely led from these specific causes to any fundamental concepts such as power, interests, freedom, sovereignty. Yet unless a student can employ such concepts he is not apt to grasp any of the problems about which he will later be expected to take some decisions. It is scarcely reassuring, for instance, to find that intelligent students, who get good marks in history, can, towards the end of their Grade 12 year, when they have studied the French Revolution and are studying the Russian Revolution, have no idea what revolutions are: no idea of the breakdown of authority, no idea of what is involved in the transfer of power from a Duma to a Soviet or of how such a transfer is possible.

Presumably this is because they have no understanding of what political authority is, have never been brought to think about what political power is for, what it does, and what conditions are necessary for its exercise. They are too busy with the names, dates, lists of unsuccessful reforms and of aims of various groups and leaders, on which they know their examination papers will be marked.

Summary of Present Defects

The main defects may be summarized as *lack of incentives*, and *presence of disincentives*: (a) for teacher and student to subordinate detailed information to a search for patterns of change, that is, to think in terms of relations of causality or interdependence of forces (e.g., the desires of individuals and groups and classes for power, for freedom, for wealth, for security, interacting on each other and with the institutions men have previously set up and with received ideas and beliefs); (b) for students to practise ordered thought of more than a few minutes' duration, such as can be induced by essay writing; (c) for students and teachers to read beyond the text-book; (*d*) for students and teachers to consider different possible interpretations of events and periods.

Sources of the Defects

The main apparent proximate source of the defects is the examination pattern. We think, however, that the examination pattern is more a symptom than a cause; it reflects, while reinforcing, the prevailing outlook and practice of teachers. The prevailing outlook and practice of teachers may be ascribed to the effective outlook and practice of the Department, in its capacity as curriculum-maker and textbook-authorizer. The official view treats history as a body of known facts and known relations between facts, which can be learned; and it demands, in any text-book seeking official approval, as much detailed factual material as (or more than) the average class and teacher can be expected to cover. This official view and practice are enough in themselves to produce the disincentives we have identified as the main trouble.

But the official view and practice are not themselves uncaused. It may be offered in extenuation of the official view and practice, that the average, or the marginal, person who teaches history in the Ontario secondary schools is incapable of the imaginative and seriously historical teaching which is wanted. If this is granted, and if it is assumed that a subject called history must be provided in the schools, the present situation is sufficiently explained. It is certainly easiest for any but the best teachers to teach, and easiest to examine students on, a body of factual material which the students can be got to extract from the text-book, and about which they can be expected to recall (the return being full marks) a requisite number of points or three out of five possible "causes" or "factors" as given on pages 171–72 of the text. The inadequacy of the teachers, and of the view and practice of the Department, reinforce each other. And the normal forces of inertia reinforce both.

The committee is of the opinion, however, that something can be done. We believe there is in the present teaching force enough latent ability, now held back by the prevailing pattern of examining and teaching, to make it worth altering the incentives and disincentives, without waiting for the day when all who teach history in the secondary schools are adequately trained historians. Improvement in the training and qualifications of those who teach history is clearly to be desired. But a start can be made before then.

A start can be made because the present defects of the teaching are not simply due to some supposed inherent inadequacy of the average teacher as now trained and recruited. Many of the defects are due to the pressures exerted on the teachers by the established school system. All the pressures direct the teachers away from scholarship. The teacher is in the classroom for (on the average) seven 40-minute periods every day, has some minor administrative tasks, and is responsible for some extra-curricular student activities. Marking papers and assignments, or reading essays, encroaches more or less heavily on his evening time. Where, in such a day, is there time, even if there were incentive, to look at historical journals or to read a new book?

Moreover, the present pressure of teaching duties is an absolute bar to any substantial move in the direction of less scrappy, i.e., more sub-jective, examinations. A teacher responsible for eight classes of 35 students (280 students), and expected to give them examinations at Christmas, Easter, and June, has 840 papers to mark during the year. Subjective papers can scarcely be marked in less than 20 minutes on the average. Papers scored objectively and/or marked on points can be marked in 5 to 10 minutes. If the extra time required for a subjective paper is reckoned at only 10 minutes, the extra time for the year's papers is 840×10 minutes: 140 hours, or, at a 6-hour marking day, 22 days. In the same way, every essay that is set, at 20 minutes' marking time, adds 280×20 minutes: 93 hours, over 15 days. Given the present teaching load, it cannot be done.

Pressure on a teacher's time is thus one of the main sources of the inadequacy of the teaching. It prevents any move away from the present defective system of examination and present paucity of student essay writing. And it prevents most teachers from reading new historical work.

The pressure on a teacher's time is not, however, the only pressure that prevents his reading. Even if this pressure were relieved there would still be, given the present ethos of school administration, little incentive for him to read. For the demands of the institution override the demands of the subject. Few principals or inspectors appear to believe that a teacher may be making as valuable a contribution to the school by doing post-graduate work as by efficient and co-operative behaviour in the school routines. A teacher gets ahead by taking part in the life of the school, not by taking time out to make himself a better historian.

No one, it may be said, is really to blame. Urban high schools are large places; they have to put hundreds or thousands of students a year through an educational process; the process gets standardized and routinized; the teachers fall into the standard pattern; the principals and inspectors keep the pattern because it is more manageable. It is easier to inspect and measure standard methods of teaching than scholarly ability. Whether the inspection is done by Departmental inspectors or by principals (and if by principals, whether directly, or indirectly by sending teachers into each others' classrooms), what is judged is the teacher's competence and dexterity in method, not his historical insight or knowledge. The system of inspection thus reinforces the other depressants of historical ability.

Recommendations

Some of the steps required to alter the pattern of teaching history and geography in the direction desired are readily apparent: some are immediately practicable, others will take longer to achieve. We suggest:

(i) A reduction in teaching load, without which the teachers cannot be expected to read in, and think about, history or geography or to confront students with different interpretations, or to set subjective examinations, or to assign and read essays and go over them with the students.

(ii) A reduction in size of classes in Grades 9 to 12. (They are already generally substantially smaller in Grade 13 than in the earlier grades.) Every class, especially in grades where a subject is compulsory, will contain slower and faster learners; hence, the larger the class, the more serious the retarding effect of the slower students.

(iii) A reduction in the total amount of detailed factual material expected to be covered, so as to allow a little more depth, more time in the classrooms for writing and for reading beyond the text-book, and more class discussion.

This will require considerable experiment (see below, point (ix)). There is necessarily a limit beyond which the reduction of detailed factual material would make interpretation and understanding nonsensical. If it were found that this limit is in fact fairly close to the present amount of detail for any given period of history or region of the world, we see only two possibilities: (1) To abandon officially the attempt to cover the present sweep, and concentrate on half the material (e.g. in Grade 9 history, instead of dashing through British history from pre-Roman times to 1900, deal only with, say, three centuries which might be thought most important, such as the seventeenth and the nineteenth; or in Grade 12 geography, not try to move through all the Eurasian countries but deal with only a few significant areas in depth). (2) To treat history and geography more seriously by giving each of them five or six periods a week instead of the present three periods in Grades 9 and 10. This would involve a history or geography option, allowing five or six periods for either instead of three periods for each. It may be objected that both history and geography are essential for every student. We think this view is fallacious. It rests on the fallacy that what is taught, however hurriedly and unmeaningfully, is learned. It would be better for students who were interested in either to have a good chance at that one subject.

It is possible that something can be done short of either of these drastic changes. The lecture system inaugurated in two Toronto schools in 1960–61 for Grade 12 history appears to have been successful. A lecture at the beginning of the week to all the Grade 12 classes, giving an over-view and raising problems, followed by discussions in the regular classrooms the rest of the week, means that less of the text-book material is covered in the standard way. Even so, when student performance was measured by an objective test (which necessarily tests material covered rather than the kind of understanding that was hoped from the lecture method), the students with whom the lecture method had been used and who had not covered some of the material in the classroom did better than the average. The lecture method has (or should have) the advantage of making more use of the best teacher. It is not a panacea: it does not turn indifferent teachers (who must still do classroom work the rest of the week) into inspired ones; but it may offer some opportunity for the routinized teacher to break away from the routine treatment. The 1960–61 experience suggests that the best third of the students become interested and read some history.

(iv) A change in the pattern of the Grade 13 examinations, as recommended above. (If Grade 13 is pulled out of the main stream and Grade 12 is made the normal school-leaving grade and is given an external examination, the same change will be needed in the Grade 12 external examination.)

(v) A change towards more subjective examinations in all the other secondary grades.

(vi) More books in the classroom, and a modest budget for academic journals and new books for the teachers' room.

(vii) An effective official recognition, at the level of inspectors, Boards, and principals, that a teacher should be more than an efficient machine in a processing industry, and should be rewarded as much for scholarship as for "efficiency" in methods. This would require a radical change in the nature and objectives of inspection.

(viii) An increase in official encouragement of teachers taking intellectual refreshment. (*a*) Provision should be made for teachers to go on paid leave to take postgraduate degree work in their subject fields, similar to the provision now made for teachers who are just short of their Type A certificate. (*b*) Encouragement of intellectual work in a teacher's subject while he is doing full-time teaching is more difficult. The initiative of the Toronto Board who, in 1961, offered a history seminar for this purpose, is clearly a step in the right direction. Yet the response to it is instructive: only a dozen teachers were interested. The small response, although all the history teachers in the Toronto secondary schools were aware that the seminar was sponsored by the Board, suggests that even in the most propitious circumstances extra work (for attendance at the seminar, unlike attendance at a few refresher lectures, requires work from all the participants) is contemplated with reluctance by teachers already sufficiently burdened. This adds weight to recommendation (i) above.

(ix) Beyond this, there is need for considerable experiment in drafting and trying out teaching courses (lessons, essay arrangements, readings, apportionment of students' time between reading, writing, listening and discussing, etc.) designed to be used with the currently authorized textbooks but to treat the material in the sort of way recommended in this report. We therefore propose that, in the first instance, the Board appoint in each of history and geography one (or more than one) experienced teacher who shares the views and the hopes of this committee, to work on a year's leave from teaching, but with such access as he needs to regular or experimental classes, to design and test such a course for one grade. Only in this way, perhaps only by repeated efforts of this sort, will it be feasible to introduce throughout the secondary school system the changes which we have argued are needed and are possible. The experiment should be extended to other grades as soon as the merit or promise of the first experiment is apparent.

Such experiments also afford the only way of finding out what concepts can be introduced (and developed) at what levels in the work of the different grades. The basic concepts of history and the social sciences are somewhat different from the basic concepts of the natural sciences: they are less certain, less divisible, less easily classifiable, less easy to arrange in a logical order of presentation. We found that the attempt could not usefully be made by a committee working in abstraction from actual school teaching, but we are convinced that it needs to be done.

Of the nine steps just listed, most (i, ii, v, vi, viii, ix,) could be carried out by Boards alone; one (iv) depends entirely on the Department; two (iii, vii) would require action by both. All of them could be undertaken without any change in the present training of the Ontario College of Education or the qualifications for certification.

For further improvement, beyond what could be expected from these steps, some improvement in the training of history teachers would be required. It would no doubt be desirable to have history taught only by historians. And no doubt there is room for improvement in the way historians (and history specialists, which is not quite the same thing) are produced in the universities and the Ontario College of Education. We do not now propose changes in the training given or the qualifications demanded, partly because no substantial change seems practicable while there is anything like the present scarcity of entrants to the profession, and partly because we think that more can be done by the steps we have proposed.

REPORT OF THE

Science Study Committee

CHARLOTTE M. SULLIVAN (CHAIRMAN)

A. D. ALLEN

R. W. MCKAY

D. G. IVEY

G. BAKER

G. HERN

L. A. SMITH

J. S. WRIGHT

NOTE: *The first three members served a full term on the summer working Committee.*

1. THE ONTARIO PROGRAMME OF STUDIES, GRADES 1-6

Comments on the Introduction

There appears to be considerable confusion in the text of the Introduction to this curriculum (1960 edition) as to the nature of science. It therefore seems worth quoting extensively from it in order to point out some of the many contradictions and to draw attention to some ideas which are alien to the spirit and methods of science.

The Introduction begins: "The course in Science is intended to include a study of the more salient features of plant and animal life, as far as possible in their natural setting— a study strictly elementary in scope yet conducted in a genuinely scientific spirit." While observation of living things in their natural setting is a part of a scientific study of nature it is necessary to recognize that scientific study frequently demands that objects to be studied be removed from their natural setting and studied under controlled conditions. It is by a combination of such investigations that reliable evidence, which forms the basis of scientific knowledge, is gathered.

"The purpose of the course is to initiate the children into the romance and wonder of science . . . ." If this means encouraging their natural curiosity about the world around them and permitting them the satisfaction of a growing understanding of natural phenomena, then it is a worth-while aim, but there is real danger that the statement may be taken to mean that children should be allowed to retain the idea that natural phenomena are inexplicable or mysterious.

"Although they are not . . . expected to amass an ordered body of scientific information, the children will, by observation, experiment and inference, learn much that will help to make richer and more significant their experience as children in a world governed by natural laws." A natural law is a statement made by man expressing or describing a certain order that he finds in nature. In order to understand a natural law it is necessary to become familiar with at least a significant part of that ordered body of information which led to the formulation of the law. In fact, the gathering of ordered bodies of information is a large part of science and is the first step in the development of valid generalizations about nature. It is not "in the unordered observation of real things and happenings that an abiding interest in science may be enkindled and the foundation laid for future systematic study. . . ." Science is possible because there is order in nature. Knowledge and understanding of science, and therefore interest in science, can be developed only as the order in nature is discovered and appreciated. The discovery of order leads to the assimilation of knowledge and encourages further observation, continued search for order, and the utilization of known order as a basis for prediction.

"Not the home, nor the school, but the unroofed country is the child's laboratory, where he finds the things which appeal to his primitive instincts." The objective, scientific study of nature is an activity of civilized man. It appeals, not to his primitive instincts, but rather to his unique intellectual faculties, of which it is a product. One of the primary aims of a curriculum in science should be the development of these faculties.

"The purpose of the course is to enhance their natural desire to get to know the world around them and find an explanation of its phenomena." At the same time "the aim will be not so much to explain phenomena as to awaken the children's interest in them and to develop their powers of accurate observation and descriptions." The second quotation contradicts the first. Observation and description are but the first steps in scientific investigation. Accurate observation is important because it helps to ensure that the next step in scientific inquiry (the questions about the observation) is relevant; it is just as important to teach children to recognize what sorts of questions or problems are within the province of science to investigate, what methods are used in the investigation, and what kinds of solutions or explanations are acceptable. To confine children's explorations of nature to observation and description, with the sole purpose of improving their competence in these skills, is to invite the destruction of their curiosity and the suppression of their natural desire to understand the world around them.

"No attempt should be made . . . to develop anything in the nature of a formal study of any particular branch of science" and yet "children should be encouraged to follow each his natural bent, to explore his favourite field and so develop a genuine interest in, and perhaps a thorough understanding of, some one phase of science." It is difficult to see how a child can be expected to understand some particular phase of science unless something in the nature of a formal study of that phase is undertaken. He is not likely to be stimulated to explore and understand unless he is guided in the methods of scientific investigation, i.e. in the ways in which factual information is gathered, correlated, and finally systematized in a body of knowledge which can be called science.

There is no intention of suggesting here that, in the primary years, students can or should be expected to gain a full appreciation of what science is, what it does, and how it does it. But if an interest in science and an understanding of its methods are considered to be among the desirable goals of education, it is essential that the proper attitudes towards science be adopted from the beginning. Although the Introduction refers to "a common core of scientific experience," there is no indication of what this common core should be. Instead, teachers are instructed to select an indefinite number of topics and activities from those listed, apparently without reference to the previous experience of the children or to whether the selection includes topics that might form part of such a core. For only one topic, health, is a definite selection of observations advocated. "The teacher should select those [activities] which have a bearing on health . . ." and should give ". . . such explanation of the principles of physiology and hygiene as may be necessary to give meaning and support to the health habits that the school attempts to establish in the lives of its pupils." The study of health and health habits already has a place in the school curriculum and it should not, therefore, also be the central theme of the science course.

Comments on the Content of the Curriculum

Any doubt whether the Introduction has been correctly interpreted or not in the foregoing discussion is dispelled by a perusal of the curriculum itself. The same unrelated activities and superficial observations are recommended year after year. Several general criticisms of the curriculum as a course in science may be made.

(i) Emphasis is almost entirely on living things. The physical and chemical nature of the environment of living things is virtually ignored, as are physical and chemical aspects of living things themselves. Living things cannot be appreciated or understood to any degree except within the context of their environment. (It is clearly unsatisfactory, for example, to discuss the need of living things for air and water, if the properties of these substances have not been discussed.) Apart from this it is far easier to grasp many of the principles common to all natural phenomena through study of inanimate matter than of much more complex animate things. Accurate information about the inanimate world should, therefore, be sought at least as zealously as information about living things.

(ii) Many of the activities listed have little or no scientific value. A few examples may be cited: making bouquets of flowers, planning and making bird baths, practising bird calls, modelling twigs, making montages, discovering how to wash woollens properly, and explaining how to feed pets.

(iii) Some of the suggested projects cannot possibly be carried out as stated, perhaps because, through looseness of wording, the statements do not properly convey what is intended; for example: "finding out why birds go south in winter" and "finding out why and how trees get rid of their leaves." Others would be extremely difficult without provision of considerably more background than is offered; for example: "demonstration of the value of woollens as insulators," "study of animals' methods of conserving body heat," "explanation of digestion as a process," and "demonstration of the value of pasteurization."

(iv) No effort is made to encourage students even to begin to recognize those similarities and differences in plant and animal types which form the basis of proper classification. No attempt is made even to consider such basic problems as how life is recognized and what distinguishes animals from plants.

(v) In every grade the course suggests that children should be told to collect things, for example, leaves, flowers, twigs with buds, coloured pictures of flowers grown from bulbs. Nothing useful is ever done, apparently, with the collections. It might be argued that further work is left to the discretion of the teacher, but entirely too much is left to the teacher.

(vi) No instructions are given to help the teacher decide what depth of treatment is expected for any of the topics listed. How can a teacher know what is to be done, or how to do it, given such vague instructions as: "recording changes of bird activities with advancing seasons," or "finding out which plants 'like' the sun," or "study of two flowering plants"?

Conclusion

The deficiencies of this course as a science course are mainly those that might be expected from the stated aims, which emphasize random observations and exclude any search for order in nature as it is revealed by observation and experimentation.

2. THE ONTARIO SCIENCE CURRICULUM, GRADES 7–10

Introduction

The intermediate division curriculum in science, published in 1961, is an improvement over the previous curriculum for this division. The emphasis on applications has been reduced and more emphasis has been placed on the treatment of topics because of their scientific importance rather than the importance of their applications.

It is difficult to consider the intermediate division of the science course by itself since the starting points in this division must be related to the level reached in previous grades. However, since the curriculum for the intermediate division has been recently revised while that for Grades 1–6 has not, no emphasis will be placed here on difficulties which might arise in the intermediate division owing to lack of continuity from the elementary to the intermediate curriculum.

The Introduction includes two aims which emphasize quite different approaches to science. Developing "an appreciation of the scientific approach to problems" and "learning something of the discoveries, content and problems of as many fields of science as possible" are both reasonable aims, but we feel that the first is by far the more important. If an attempt is made to give a broad survey of science in the limited time available, it may not be possible to develop the primary aim, which is an understanding of the nature of science.

It is our view that the proper way to develop an understanding of science is to treat certain fundamental topics thoroughly, so that the principles involved are made clear, and then to build on this knowledge by consideration of ways in which these principles underlie specific topics in any branch of science. This approach would necessitate the removal of much of the material in the present course in order to provide adequate time to treat the rest of it properly. Some of the material removed could well be treated in earlier grades.

The Treatment of Central Principles

I. CENTRAL PRINCIPLES

A few ideas are of fundamental importance in the various phases of science. These ideas should, therefore, be developed early and their importance should be stressed continuously throughout the course as various topics involving them are discussed. This is not done in the present course. The following are examples of such ideas:

(i) ENERGY. The concept of energy, and its underlying importance in all physical, chemical and biological systems, is probably the most important single concept to be developed. Topics which could be treated under this heading are: the various forms of energy; transformation of energy from one form to another; conservation of energy; the ultimate degradation of all energy into heat energy; interdependence of living things and the dependence of all life on energy from the sun.

(ii) PROPERTIES OF MATTER. Matter should be classified and its properties described quantitatively wherever possible. Discussions under this heading could include: the general properties of the three states of matter; the characteristic properties of matter (e.g., density, conductivity, specific heat, vapour pressure and boiling point) and the dependence, if any, of these properties on such variables as temperature and pressure; the atomic nature of matter, and the kinetic theory of heat; the nature and properties of solutions; the tendency of atoms to combine, and the associated energy changes.

(iii) BIOLOGY. Certain biological principles should be kept in mind as guides to introductory studies. Among the most important of these are: reproduction, with associated growth and differentiation, which implies continuity of living systems through time as described by the Cell Theory; variability, heredity and natural selection, which lead to the theory of evolution as a way of accounting for the geological record of life on this planet and the diversity of organisms.

II. TREATMENT OF THESE PRINCIPLES

(i) ENERGY. In this curriculum the basic ideas of energy are not dealt with until late in the course (10.4),* so that the earlier discussion of heat must be based on intuitive ideas of energy which will be vague and may be wrong. Magnetism (7.4) and sound (9.1) are discussed without reference to energy. Similarly biological processes for which the concept of energy is important are discussed before energy is studied; for example: movement of water into roots and up stems (7.1), photosynthesis (7.1, 9.4), cellular respiration (9.4), and nutrition (9.7).

(ii) PROPERTIES OF MATTER: PHYSICAL PROPERTIES. The course includes some discussion of changes of state (7.2, 9.3, 10.5), thermal expansion (7.3), density (9.2), specific heat (10.5), solutions and mixtures (7.2, 9.3). Some criticisms are: (*a*) Change of state is discussed before the properties of the various states of matter, which are only briefly mentioned (9.3). Apart from an optional item (9.3), no attempt is made to use a molecular model to describe these properties. The discussion is almost entirely concerned with water, which is not a typical substance. (*b*) No mention is made of the effect of temperature on density, although this is needed to explain convection (7.3). (*c*) With one optional exception (9.3), discussions of solutions deal only with solutions in water, and the general nature of solutions is not discussed. (*d*) Evaporation (7.1, 7.2, 9.3), diffu-

*References such as (10.4) refer to Grade and Unit, for example, 10.4 means Grade 10, Unit 4.

sion, and osmosis (9.4) are discussed without reference to the kinetic theory.

PROPERTIES OF MATTER: CHEMICAL PROPERTIES. The topics which form an introduction to chemistry are: air (8.4), air and the properties of its components (9.3), solutions (7.2, 9.3), chemical energy (10.8), and some properties of oxides (10.8). The first chemical reactions that are mentioned as such are the burning of various materials in oxygen (air), and the preparation and properties of oxygen and carbon dioxide. None of these reactions can be discussed usefully without some background, which is not provided. They are introduced not because they are suitable introductory experiments in chemistry but because the gases happen to occur in air. First experiments should be concerned with reactants and products which are readily recognized and studied, and should not involve gases.

(iii) BIOLOGY. *Reproduction* in plants is studied in some detail, but in animals it is merely noted in connection with their life histories. The distinction between vegetative and sexual reproduction in plants (8.1) is not made clear until Grade 10 (10.1). The fact that reproduction implies the continuity of life, through time, is not suggested as an important conclusion to be drawn from studies of reproduction of organisms.

Cell Theory is badly neglected in the curriculum. First mention of cells is made in (8.2), where protozoans are introduced as "one-celled" animals and it is suggested that their functions be compared with those of "multi-celled" animals. Neither cells, nor the cellular nature of organisms, are mentioned again until 9.4. In subsequent studies in Grade 9 some attempt is made to keep before the students the fact that cells are the structural and functional units of animals. This emphasis is not continued in the study of plants in Grade 10.

The second part of the cell theory—that new living cells can arise only by reproduction from living cells—is not mentioned, and again an opportunity for discussing the continuity of living things is lost.

The concepts of *variability* and *natural selection* as factors in the evolution of living things could very well be introduced in a study of selected examples of adaptations, but only if students become familiar with the basic structural patterns which have been adapted. The horse's hoof or the bird's wing as adaptations for running or flying are studied without reference to the basic pentadactyl vertebrate limb.

The mechanisms by which *evolution* of living forms occurs cannot be advantageously discussed at this level, but there are many opportunities, of which no use is made, for discussion of evidence for evolution in the biological and geological material studied.

Conservation

Intelligent management of our renewable natural resources must be based upon an understanding of the principles of conservation of matter and the irreversible degradation of energy to heat which determine the interdependence of living things and their dependence on their environment. Conservation receives considerable emphasis during Grades 7–10 in such topics as the water cycle (7.2), forests (7.8), soil (8.7), balance of nature (8.8), plant communities and successions (10.3), but the essential concepts are lacking. As a result of the treatment given to these topics the reasons for conservation that seem likely to emerge are that our plant and animal resources are useful because they lend themselves to economic and recreational exploitation by man. Conservation studies based on this approach properly belong in the geography course and should not be given such an amount of time in a science course as they receive here.

Quantitative Treatment

There is too little quantitative work in this course. Problems are prescribed only on velocity of sound, quantity of heat, electric circuits, and work. None of these topics occurs before Grade 9.

Some simple measurements could be introduced in Grades 7 and 8 in connection with topics now in the course, for example, solubility, composition of solutions or mixtures. Other topics which could quite simply be treated quantitatively might be introduced in Grades 7 and 8, such as uniform motion, density, etc. If students became accustomed to applying the arithmetic they are taught at or before this level they would have less difficulty in Grades 9 and 10 in using the mathematics they are then taught.

Science is quantitative, and mathematics is frequently referred to as the language of science. Emphasis should be placed on algebraic equations as concise statements of ideas rather than merely mechanical aids to solving problems.

Modern Science

"The wider dissemination of scientific knowledge by all media of mass communication and education means that younger pupils are becoming familiar, even if only superficially, with many aspects of modern science. The interest that has been thus aroused makes many topics teachable, and their teaching imperative, which formerly were thought to be suitable only for more mature minds. If advantage is not taken of this immediate interest, golden opportunities are lost." These sentences appear on pages 4–5 of the curriculum. However, in this course, hardly any concepts originating within the last hundred years are included, except for the mention of electrons, hydrogen bombs, and nuclear energy. The choice of the last two items indicates a tendency to confuse science and technology.

The stated aim to include topics from modern science and the virtual absence of modern science from the course emphasize the fact that a careful preparation is necessary before modern science can be appreciated. By employing an approach in which basic principles are emphasized the intermediate course could go much further towards providing such a preparation, and this is all that should be attempted at this stage.

Comments on Individual Sections

ANIMAL KINGDOM (8.2). The preface to this unit contains the statement that "this is a comparative study intended to encourage the pupil to . . . notice the characteristics that form the basis of scientific classification of the animal kingdom." The intention of making a comparative study is, however, frustrated by the fact that different things are selected for study in each of the animal types. For example: (*a*) excretion is selected for study in protozoans but not in any other animal; (*b*) breathing is studied in molluscs but not in other types; (*c*) the jointed structure of the body of millipedes or centipedes is observed but it is not compared with the body structure of other animals; (*d*) exoskeleton is noted in arthropods but not in molluscs, nor is attention drawn to the absence of exoskeleton in "worms" (annelids).

The intention of familiarizing students with the characteristics which form the basis for scientific classification is not consistently carried out. For example, the general characteristics of various vertebrate classes are studied but the common characteristics which place them in the Phylum Chordata are virtually ignored. On the other hand considerable time is devoted to classifying some animals according to characteristics which have no bearing on "scientific classification." Thus birds are classified in three ways, according to what they eat, where they live, and their seasonal behaviour.

In this connection it might be noted that, in spite of extensive studies of plants in Grades 7–10, the bases for classifying the major groups are never properly established.

BIOLOGY (9.5, 9.6, 9.7). Observations on a variety of invertebrate and vertebrate animals in (9.5) and (9.6) are confined to external anatomical details and discussions of life histories. Internal organization is mentioned only in connection with the function of the circulatory system in transport of respiratory gases. The structure and functions of other systems in any of the animals studied are not discussed nor is any use made of dissected specimens. But (9.7) calls for study, in considerable detail of the anatomy and functions of several organ systems of man, which of necessity must be done entirely from charts and diagrams.

This kind of study of man without similar studies of other animals is a serious error for two reasons: (a) it is assumed that students will be able to visualize the organization of human organ systems and understand the role they play in the economy of the organism without ever having seen, or discussed the functions of, any of these organ systems in any other animal; (b) a fundamental precept in science teaching, that students should learn so far as possible from first hand observation and that they should be led to generalizations on the basis of their observations, is virtually ignored.

SOUND (9.1). Parts 1 and 3 of this unit, entitled "The Propagation of Sound" and "Characteristics of Sound," could be taught by themselves, but they would mean much more if they were preceded by a study of waves. Part 2, "Sound Waves," is apparently intended to provide this introduction but, in fact, confuses waves with vibrations and does not refer to simple, visible examples of wave motion. The discussion of sound as due to vibration of molecules is a poor choice for the first reference to molecules in the course.

ELECTRICITY (10.7). The emphasis on electrons in this unit seems rather inconsistent in a course where atoms and molecules are merely referred to in passing and atomic structure is not mentioned. The suggestion that the student should study "The movement of electrons as illustrated by sparks" is meaningless.

CHEMICAL ENERGY (10.8). The topics listed as an introduction to chemical energy are photosynthesis, the voltaic cell, oxidation, and nuclear reactions (optional). Photosynthesis is far too complex to serve as an introduction to chemical energy, and nuclear reactions are not examples of chemical energy.

Treatment of these selected topics gives the impression that only certain types of chemical reactions produce or consume energy. The selection is apparently based on applications (of chemical energy) without regard to the need to introduce the subject simply and logically. There is no indication that every chemical reaction involves energy changes.

Summary

Lack of consistency in selection and treatment of topics, and failure to relate the topics treated to a core of basic principles, detract seriously from the value of this curriculum. The random survey of too wide a range of material must lead to memorization of unrelated facts and statements rather than to an understanding of their significance or of the scientific principles involved. Some attempt to teach the background necessary for an appreciation of modern science would be far more useful than the isolated mention of a few applications such as nuclear energy and the atomic bomb.

3. THE ONTARIO COURSES OF STUDY IN SCIENCE, GRADES 11–13

Introduction

Our comments regarding the Ontario courses of study in Physics, Chemistry, Botany, and Zoology for Grades 11, 12, and 13 are not as extensive as our discussions of the science courses for the elementary and intermediate divisions. We feel that detailed criticisms would be out of order because it is evident that most of the senior division science courses will have to be revised in the near future as a consequence of the fact that many of the topics at present listed for these courses are included in the new intermediate division Science Syllabus. This report then consists of but a few general comments.

Grades 12 and 13 Chemistry

Most of the Grade 12 course is qualitative and much of it could have been covered in earlier grades. The rapid introduction of too many new ideas at this level makes it difficult for the student to assimilate them into his thinking and to make generalizations from them. A more gradual introduction over several previous grades would be very beneficial, so that, by Grade 12, the student would be familiar with a variety of chemical elements and compounds, with the nature of chemical reactions and the associated energy changes, and with the importance of atomic structure.

The Grade 12 course does not include atomic structure, the way in which atoms combine, or the energy changes involved. The chemical bond is introduced "as a convenient method of illustrating valence" only. The treatment given for individual elements, families of elements, and compounds does not lead to an understanding of their chemical properties.

The Grade 13 course deals very inadequately with such topics as reaction rates, equilibria, atomic structure, ionization, and solutions. The chemical bond is briefly mentioned, and the energy associated with bond formation is ignored. Some groups of elements are dealt with in some detail, but the essential nature of each element and its dependence on atomic structure is not brought out. The section on organic compounds does not develop the ideas of stereochemistry and the characteristic properties of functional groups, on which the major part of this subject depends.

In general, far too much unrelated information is given in these courses (preparation and properties of too many compounds, complex reactions treated superficially, and crude details of industrial processes). The result is that an average student, faced in so short a time with a bewildering mass of new factual material, resorts to memorizing these facts and gains little or no insight into the nature of chemistry. These courses form a poor background, both for students who intend to continue their studies and for those who do not. The knowledge gained is superficial and unrelated, and is consequently soon forgotten.

Grades 11 and 13 Physics

No detailed criticism of the Grade 11 and Grade 13 physics curricula will be given here, but two comments may be useful.

(i) The study of electrolysis and voltaic cells in Grade 11, with no previous introduction to chemistry, is of doubtful value. Either an adequate foundation for these topics should precede them or they should be postponed for later consideration. Since the definition of the International Ampere, based on electrolysis, has been obsolete for twenty years and since the voltaic cell is now only one of many sources of electric energy, postponement of any study of electrochemistry would not be unreasonable.

(ii) The Grade 13 course should provide some introduction to topics in modern physics. However, the opportunity to do so is lost in the present course because emphasis has been placed on a miscellaneous group of technical applications instead of on the important theoretical significance of the experiments done. For example, the study of spectra leads to chemical analysis rather than to basic ideas of atomic structure, the study of the photoelectric effect ends in discussion of exposure meters rather than the Einstein equation, and the study of electronics involves exceedingly complicated practical devices but does not refer to measurement of the electronic charge or mass.

Grade 13 *Botany and Zoology*

A large proportion of the subject-matter of these courses will now be covered in the intermediate division Science and it is clear that new courses for Grade 13 will have to be introduced.

It is to be hoped that in these new courses emphasis will be shifted from nineteenth-century descriptive biology to twentieth-century biology. In this connection it may be pointed out that much of modern biology requires as a foundation certain physical and chemical concepts. Revised courses in these related sciences should include those fundamental ideas which are a necessary basis for exploring and understanding some modern biological problems.

4. AN APPROACH TO A NEW SCIENCE COURSE

Introduction

In our scientific civilization every educated person finds his outlook influenced by science: "The effects of science on human life and thought have become so great, and are potentially so much greater, that those who have no understanding of them, and of the science which has produced them, cannot be considered properly educated or truly cultured and therefore are unable to participate fully in the life of their time. Present scientific illiteracy is, in part, due to a lack of factual knowledge, but is much more the result of a lack of understanding of the basic nature and aims of science." (*Science and Education: A Policy Statement* by The Science Masters Association and The Association of Women Science Teachers; London: Murray, 1961.) The importance of science teaching is stressed from a slightly different point of view in another statement which may be quoted: "Economic stability, public welfare and maintenance of a free society are intimately related to the discoveries of science . . . More than a casual acquaintance with scientific enterprise is essential to effective citizenship." ("Rethinking Science Education," Paul de H. Hurd in the

1960 *Year Book* of the National Society for Study of Education.) Science teaching in our schools must be designed to give all students the understanding of science which they need to take their places effectively in our scientific civilization.

A second purpose of a science curriculum must be to interest potential scientists in scientific careers, and to give them a sound foundation for further training.

At least in the elementary and intermediate divisions there is no essential difference between the courses of study necessary for these two purposes. For the future scientist as well as for all others the first essential is an understanding of the nature of science. A certain body of factual information is necessary for developing an understanding of science, but acquisition of such information should not be made an end in itself.

General Remarks

The basic principles that must be used as a guide to the construction of a course in science have been discussed to some extent in our criticism of the Ontario curricula. The primary aim of the course should be to develop an understanding of the nature of science and its methods. We feel that the only way to achieve this is to treat certain fundamental ideas thoroughly, and to emphasize their significance by consideration of the ways in which they underlie specific topics in any branch of science. It is important that these fundamental ideas should be so well developed and illustrated throughout the course that they become ingrained in the thinking of the student. The selection of individual topics to be studied should be based to a large extent on their appropriateness for the development of these ideas.

Ideas required early in the study of science cannot be presented fully when first introduced. They should be used again and again whenever they assist in the development of other ideas, and their meaning should be more completely explained as the student's increasing maturity makes this possible. In this way one might hope to build up a core of essential ideas which are retained and used by the student throughout his whole career.

One valuable method of emphasizing the importance of these central ideas is to integrate, as fully as possible, not only the branches of science but also science and such closely allied subjects as mathematics and social studies. Quantitative work in science should be introduced as soon as the student is capable of handling the numbers involved. In some cases it may be necessary to introduce in the science course some simple mathematical concepts which would help in the development of the subject, but it is also highly desirable that many of the examples used for practice in mathematics should be drawn from science. We feel sure that both subjects would benefit from this, since it would emphasize both the quantitative nature of science and the universal usefulness of mathematics.

Certain topics are frequently included in school science courses simply because they have some practical application. While there can be no general objection to the inclusion of such topics, it is important that the reason for their inclusion should be that they illustrate some principle that is being discussed. Too frequently applications which are included purely for the sake of interest involve principles which are too complex to be understood by the students, and their treatment becomes a superficial discussion of meaningless names and phrases. If this passes for an understanding of the subject then a completely wrong attitude is developed in the student. One of the aims of science education is to produce adults who can distinguish between statements which are capable of proof and vague statements which appear plausible but which have no basis in fact. If people are to be able to make reasonable judgments of the validity of information given to them, they must not be exposed in school to inadequate or inaccurate "explanations" of complex phenomena which they cannot possibly understand but which they must commit to memory and repeat as gospel truths in an examination.

In addition to the topics which must be included because they help in the development of fundamental ideas, there will be others which may be included at various stages because they relate to the students' interests. It is most important, however, that the treatment of these topics should not be a mere repetition of what a student has already learned outside the school. Many of the early experiments with magnets are examples of this. If a student's interest demands that a subject be treated, then the treatment must build on that interest, particularly with regard to classifying, ordering, and extending the information previously gathered. If students can be taught to look for order in the information they are continually acquiring, both in and out of school, then the basis of a good scientific attitude will have been laid and the process of learning new facts will have been made much easier.

If some new topics are to be included and others are to be given a much fuller treatment than previously, then much of the material in present courses must be removed. Trying to cover too many different topics inevitably results in an inadequate treatment of all of them. As a consequence of this the student rarely achieves a proper understanding of any one topic.

It may be suggested that the type of curriculum proposed will benefit only the very good student and that the average student will find too high hurdles placed in his path by the emphasis on the introduction of fundamental principles at an early stage in the course. We do not believe that this criticism is warranted, although experimental trials of the sort of course proposed would be needed to settle this and other questions. The very brilliant student shows a remarkable tendency to learn in spite of both poor teaching and poor choice of topics, possibly because he finds for himself the order which correlates the random ideas with which he is confronted. The average or below average student, in similar conditions, becomes lost and is forced to resort to uncomprehending memorization. If the content of the course is restricted so that time is provided for consideration of important principles, and topics are chosen in such a way as to form a coherent system, the average student would be greatly assisted in attaining an understanding of science which is practically denied him at present. The proposed approach should greatly benefit the very good student as well but it is not designed primarily for him.

In the literature on science education, emphasis is often placed on "the scientific method." Either directly or by implication this method is said to consist of carrying out experiments and drawing conclusions from them. This inductive procedure is of great importance both in research and in teaching, but it has no exclusive claim to be called *the* scientific method. There are many topics which can be treated much more clearly in the reverse order, i.e. a principle or axiom is stated, certain consequences are deduced, and these consequences are then compared with the results of experiment. As an example we may consider the atomic nature of matter. One might begin with experiments dealing with composition of compounds, infer the laws of constant and multiple proportions and then proceed, as Dalton did, to theories of atoms and molecules. On the other hand one might begin by postulating the existence of atoms and molecules and then discuss the consequences of this theory in connection with many topics such as states of matter, kinetic theory, solutions, and chemical combination. Both methods require reference to experimental results and both methods are valid approaches to the topic. For this particular problem, however, the second approach is much more flexible and allows the teacher to make use of the illuminating ideas of atoms and molecules much sooner than would be possible by the first method. Both inductive and deductive methods in a variety of forms have a place in the study of science and no undue emphasis should be placed on a single scientific method.

Studies by other Groups

This committee has been able to make a brief study of several science curricula from other areas. The general concern that is felt over the inadequacy of science education is shown by the many attempts that have been made to devise new curricula. None of the new curricula for the elementary and intermediate grades that we have seen meets the need for the balanced, sequential treatment of topics that we feel is essential. The difficulties to be overcome in devising such a course are obviously very great. Close co-operation between specialists, both in the various branches of science and in education, will be necessary, and a great deal of experimental classroom work will be required.

For the senior grades the courses of study issued in the United States by the Biological Sciences Curriculum Study group, the Physical Sciences Study Committee, the Chemical Bond Approach Committee, and the CHEM Study Group are very valuable contributions and deserve serious consideration. Proposed new courses for the teaching of biology, physics and chemistry in grammar schools in the United Kingdom are described in a series of pamphlets issued jointly by the Science Masters Association and the Association of Women Science Teachers. These studies should be of great assistance when the task of revising Ontario Curricula is undertaken.

Other Problems

Many important questions which demand serious study are not discussed in this report. We felt that it was more useful to concentrate, in the limited time available, on a careful statement of curriculum requirements rather than on a wider range of problems. Some topics which we have not attempted to deal with are: selection or preparation of text-books, teaching manuals and teaching aids; training of teachers (in-service and pre-service); the relation of science to mathematics, Social Studies, English, etc.; the advisability of having science specialists below the Grade 7 level; the kind of organization needed to prepare new programmes in science.

Outline of a Course in Science

The fundamental ideas of energy, matter, and life must form the basis of a satisfactory course in science. The development of these ideas and the

GRADES 1, 2		The earth as a rotating sphere Day and night	Naming and examining representativ Metals, plastics, wood, bone, shells, rocks, soils, sand, bricks, concrete, glass Water, oils, cleaning fluid Air, natural gas
			Noting similarities and difference between living and non-living thing: have come from living things. Rec
GRADES 3, 4	The earth as a planet Length of days at different times of year Solar system. Moon	Forces: muscular, elastic, gravita- tional, and frictional Weight and size (3)* Work Energy of position (Note A)	Evaporation and condensation (1) Solutions of solids in liquids; recovery by evaporation (2) Evaporation as solution of water in air Effect of moving air on rate of evaporation (1)
GRADES 5, 6	Stars and navigation The sun as a star Energy from the sun (6)	Energy and motion Friction and heat Kinetic theory of heat Temperature; thermometers (4) Radiant energy from hot bodies (6) Heat conduction (Note A)	Particulate nature of matter; motion of particles in gases (free), in liquids (limited by mutual attraction), in solids (vibration) Existence of some materials in several states (e.g. ice, water, steam) Solutions, saturation (kinetic treatment) Solution of gases in liquids (7) Vapour content of air at different temperatures (8) Effect of evaporation on temperature
GRADES 7, 8	Phases of the moon Seasonal changes of temperature	Graphs (distance- time and speed- time) Density Thermal expansion Convection in fluids (9) Pressure in gasses (kinetic theory) Barometer Boyle's law	Common elements: copper, iron, zinc, mercury, carbon, sulphur, oxygen, nitrogen, hydrogen Reactions of elements to form com- pounds (ZnS, FeS, CuS, HgS). Conservation of mass Atomic arrangements in elements and compounds. Use of models Similarity between oxygen and sulphur; formation of oxides Composition of air (tests for components) (10) (Note C)
GRADES 9, 10	Specific heat Changes of state, heats of fusion and vaporization Vapour pressure, boiling and melting points Charles' law, general gas laws Diffusion and osmosis (Note D) Electric and magnetic energy Electromagnetic waves, light Conservation of energy. Degradation of other forms of energy to heat energy (11)		Review of chemical reactions, energy, atomic arrangements Introduction to atomic structure, atomic weights, periodicity, valency, and the chemical bond

*Certain topics from the various categories of subjects have been indicated by identical numbers in

materials, plants and animals. Animals with back bones; examples from each class, noting external covering, limbs, eyes, etc. Animals without back bones: worms, snails, insects, etc. Green plants: ferns and flowering plants Non-green plants: mushrooms, moulds leading to classification. Distinguishing Noting that some non-living things ognizing solids, liquids, and gases.	Wind as air in motion Wind moves clouds		
Plants need water, air, constituents from soil (2), light Moisture from plants—transpiration (1) Animals need water, air, food Moisture in breath (1); perspiration (1) Movement—muscular force, work, energy (3); movement as a characteristic of living organisms (Note B)	Classification continued Simple external anatomy of plants and animals Germination of seeds; hatching of eggs (descriptive); life cycles (descriptive) Growth and differentiation as characteristics of living organisms	Clouds, rain, and fog (1)	Soluble matter in soils (2)
Plants need light—radiant energy (6) Water and solute transport in plants Evaporation of water from leaves (2) Movement. Limbs as levers; movement in relation to energy Muscular energy does work, or changes to heat Temperature as a stimulus, temperature sense (4), (6) Other stimuli, other senses (6) Response of plants to light Respiration in water (7) (Note B)	Classification continued Plant anatomy: flower detail, fruits, seeds Reproduction, growth, and differentiation Continuity of life and history of life on earth (5)	Air temperature (4) Evaporation and condensation in relation to weather (8) Water cycle	Igneous and sedimentary rocks Erosion. Deposition of sediments Fossils History of life (5)
Cells as units of function Requirements of green plants: light, water, nutrients, CO_2, O_2; net loss of O_2, consumption of CO_2 in light; consumption of O_2, loss of CO_2 in dark (10) Requirements of animals: food, water, O_2; elimination of CO_2 (10) Balanced aquaria. Dependence of animals on plants, plants on (sun) light (6), (10) Blood pigments in transport of O_2	Classification continued Internal anatomy of plants; gross anatomy of a few animals—digestive, circulatory, breathing, and nervous systems Cellular nature of organisms	Wind systems, convection (9)	
Functions related to structures (details only as far as progress in development of physical and chemical concepts permits) Conservation of matter and one-way flow of energy in food webbs (general treatment) (11) Diffusion, osmosis, convection, and conduction in transport of materials in plants and animals	Review and complete classification to major phyla, some classes and orders and a few genera Gross anatomy, external and internal (comparative) Introduction to study of adaptations, to struggle for survival (i.e., natural selection), and to heredity Microscopic study of cell structure Organization of cells into tissues, tissues into organs, organs into organ systems		

parentheses to show that they present opportunities for correlation.

relationships between them should be the central theme of the course. In the limited time available we have been able to do no more than outline a possible approach to the development of these ideas. For Grades 1–10 we have drawn up a scheme (see chart) in which a parallel treatment of topics is indicated. Some sections of this scheme have been expanded to show in more detail how they might be treated. These appear as Notes A, B, C, and D in the appendix.

The last three grades are covered less fully, since the range of topics from which a selection might be made is much broader. In our opinion it is desirable that Physics courses be given in Grades 11 and 13, Chemistry in 12 and 13, and Biology in 12 and 13 and that it should be possible for students intending to follow a career in science to take all six courses and also Mathematics.

PHYSICS, Grades 11 and 13

The physics courses for Grades 11 and 13 might well be based on the course developed by the Physical Sciences Study Committee. This course consists of four parts. Part I (The Universe) and Part II (Optics and Waves) could be taught in Grade 11 or sooner, and Part III (Mechanics) and Part IV (Electricity and Atomic Structure) in Grade 13.

It might be pointed out that some of the mathematical concepts needed in teaching physics are introduced in the PSSC course. This is a practical way of providing the necessary mathematical tools. However, it might be more desirable to modify the mathematics courses in such a way as to make this expedient unnecessary.

CHEMISTRY, Grades 12 and 13

The fundamental idea which underlies the whole of chemistry is the nature of the chemical bond. Discussions of chemical bonding should include the stereochemistry of elements and compounds, the energies associated with bond formation and rupture, and the nature of the particles formed when bonds are broken, particularly when these are stabilized by solvent action. These discussions must be based on the structure of atoms and the energies associated with loss and gain of electrons. When this basis has been laid, meaningful discussions can be given of such topics as the nature of solutions, acids and bases, and the general properties of compounds such as chemical composition, physical properties, and stereochemistry.

In this kind of treatment a large body of related facts and information can be given to the students without making impossible demands on their memory. The principles behind some industrial processes can also be included.

BIOLOGY, Grades 12 and 13

Biological principles and their applications should form the core of the Biology programme for Grades 12 and 13. It is these principles which unify the science of living organisms and an understanding of them enables a student to interpret and integrate new phenomena into his general body of knowledge and experience.

It has been argued that young students cannot cope with principles because they lack the necessary physical and chemical concepts as well as the essential biological facts from which the principles follow. This argument should not apply to the courses outlined here, in part because the programme for Grades 1–10 will have supplied a solid body of biological facts as well as some of the essential physical and chemical concepts, and in part because the sequence and content of the science courses proposed for Grades 11–13 would be designed to ensure that further essential physical and chemical concepts are introduced either before or as they are needed for biological studies. Thus it is envisioned that although the sciences are separated in Grades 11, 12, and 13, those concepts which are common to all of them will not be lost to view.

A great deal of time and thought would be required to plan the Biology programme in detail. It is appropriate here to make only very general suggestions as to its content. These suggestions are: (*a*) Concept of organism—organization, metabolism, regulatory mechanisms; (*b*) Ecological principles—the interdependence of organisms, the interrelation of organism and environment, population dynamics; (*c*) Principles of reproduction—patterns of reproduction, embryology, regulation of differentiation; (*d*) Principles of genetics—heredity and variability, mechanisms of gene action; (*e*) Principles of natural selection and theory of evolution.

The development of satisfactory courses for the senior grades will not be an easy task, but in some ways it will be simpler than the introduction of good science courses in the earlier grades. Several studies have already been made, and while none of them meets our needs completely, much help can be derived from them. Great improvements can be made by simply changing the courses in Grades 11, 12 and 13, but far better results will be achieved when a background of scientific experience is provided in the earlier grades.

APPENDIX

Note A: *Introduction to Energy* (Grades 3–6)

MUSCULAR FORCES

Pulling, pushing, lifting various objects as examples of *exerting a force*.
Equality of action and reaction.
Forces make objects move.
Forces stop moving objects.

    Examples: Throwing and catching a ball.
           Sliding an object on a smooth table.
           Sliding an object on ice.
           Pulling and stopping a wagon or a roller-skate, etc.

Balanced forces do not make objects move, e.g., two boys pushing opposite sides of wagon.

OTHER FORCES

Elastic Forces
Sling-shot, bow and arrow, coiled spring.
Motion of shot or arrow.
No motion when *elastic force* balanced by *muscular force*.

Gravity (Weight)
Object released falls—must be a downward force.
Object held in hand does not fall (balancing downward force by muscular force).
Lifting various objects. Muscular force greater for larger objects of same material; muscular force greater for lead or iron than for wood of same size.
Downward pull called *weight*.
Downward pull called *force of gravity*.
Downward meaning towards centre of earth (relate to earth as a sphere, people not falling off China).
Weighing as measure of gravitational force. Plotting weight *v.* time for students, or pets.

Friction
Sliding objects stop (less quickly on ice).
Rolling objects stop less quickly.
Friction is the force causing objects to stop.
Friction balances small forces and prevents movement starting.

WORK AND ENERGY

Examples of Work
Shovelling earth into truck.
Lifting·objects from floor to table.
Pushing objects across table.
We do *work* when we move an object against a force.
We use muscular energy to do *work*.

Energy of Position
Boys on see-saw (levers) or weights on string over pulley.
   When one goes down, other goes up.
   Work is done on the *rising* boy or weight.
   Work is done by the other. Hardly any muscular energy used.
Energy of position used to do work.
Object at greater height has more *energy of position*.
When weight is lifted from floor to table *muscular energy* produces energy
    of position.
When object is pushed against friction, muscular energy is used but does
    not increase energy of position. (Brief discussion of friction and heat
    introducing topic dealt with in Grades 5 and 6.)

Energy of Motion
Bouncing ball; energy of position at top; energy of motion at bottom. Two
    kinds of energy changing back and forth, one to other. Some mech-
    anical energy lost on each bounce (heat produced).
Weight on a spring vibrating up and down.
Pendulum; energy changes, air resistance. Pendulum with baffle to increase
    air resistance.
Throwing a ball; muscular energy to energy of motion.
Sliding object coming to rest; energy of motion to heat.

REVIEW, MECHANICAL ENERGY

Energy of position—gravitational, elastic (bow, sling-shot).
Energy of motion.

HEAT AS A FORM OF ENERGY

Mechanical energy to heat (rubbing sticks, hack saw, brake-drums).
Kinetic theory of heat (related to parallel discussion of particulate nature
    of matter).
Heat is energy of random motion.

TEMPERATURE

Related to direction of heat transfer between substances in contact.

Temperature scales degrees C, degrees F.

Discussion of air temperature in summer, winter, of temperature of sun, etc.

Presence of heat energy in cold objects as well as hot; i.e., heat can flow from ice at 32° F to ice at 0° F and from ice at 0° F to colder ice.

NOTE B: *A suggested treatment of those aspects of Biology which should be integrated with physical-chemical studies for Grades 3–6*

There are two separate lines of development in the suggested course in Biology—one deals with kinds of organisms and their organization, gradually building up a knowledge of the variety of organisms, their gross structure, their functions, and life histories, and the other interprets vital functions of living organisms in terms of physical and chemical concepts. This note is confined to the latter material. There are two sections in what follows: Section I, containing material which is related to studies of evaporation, condensation and solutions; Section II, suggesting how studies of force and energy might be correlated with certain biological studies.

SECTION I

Plants and animals need water

Effects of depriving plants of water.

Transpiration (evaporation of water from leaves); collection by condensation.

Discussion of need for water by humans, pets.

Demonstration of moisture in breath, collected by condensation.

Discussion of moisture lost as perspiration; its evaporation into air; effect of moving air on rate of evaporation of moisture from skin.

Plants and animals need air

Comparison of growth of plants in sealed and unsealed containers.

Survival of flies in sealed and unsealed tubes.

Plants need constituents from the soil

Extraction of soluble materials from soil; filtration of solution and evaporation of filtrate to show presence of soluble materials.

Extraction of clean (acid washed) sand, filtration and evaporation to show absence of soluble material.

Growth of plants in clean sand, sand with soil solutes added, and soil itself to demonstrate differences in growth.

Water and solute transport in plants

Growing plants in coloured water. A variety of demonstrations showing that solution moves up stems and into leaves.

Collection of transpired water, evaporated to discover that water transpired contains no solutes.

Discussion in general terms of the use made by plants of soluble soil constituents.

Animals need food

Kinds of food that various animals eat; trace source of animal food back to plants.

Respiration in water

Gases (air) dissolve in water.

Aquatic organisms (fish, frogs, snails, earthworm) need this dissolved air just as land animals need air around them.

Demonstration of effects of depriving aquatic plants and animals of air.

SECTION II

Movement is characteristic of living things

Animals move. They can pull, push, lift objects; they can *exert a force*.

Equality of action and reaction, e.g., push box forward along floor— observe push of feet back against floor and push of floor against feet; box loaded with books requires greater push than empty box. Relate to friction. Relate to walking, walking on ice, running, swimming; to locomotion of animals such as fish, frog, earthworm, crayfish, etc.

Organisms have weight; they are acted upon by a downward force (gravity); they fall.

Organisms get heavier as they grow. Larger objects are heavier than smaller objects of the same material. Keep weight-time charts and graphs of students, classroom animals.

Muscles of animals exert force; larger muscles can exert greater force, lift heavier objects than smaller ones. Muscles get larger as animal grows.

Muscles exert a force—can do work. Muscular energy can be changed into other kinds of energy—e.g., energy of position, of motion, of heat.

Plants move—can do work, e.g., movement of plant stems against gravity (experiments on response of roots and stems to gravity).

Plants can exert a force, do work (experiments on force exerted by growing plants).

Muscles can exert force, only when they contract. On contraction they move one part in relation to another part—e.g., lower arm in relation to upper arm, fingers in relation to lower arm; study other animals.

Limbs as levers.

Principle of antagonistic pairs of muscles—e.g., arm muscles, muscles of frog, fish, etc.

Conversion of muscular energy to work, heat. Running—muscular energy does work; some energy is converted directly to heat, runner becomes warmer.

Energy is used in growth—some is lost by direct conversion to heat. (Grow seedlings and observe rise in temperature in substrate.)

Heat in animals and plants, as in non-living matter, is energy of random motion of particles.

Particulate nature of animals and plants.

Temperature and temperature sense, other stimuli and senses

Direction of heat transfer between hand and cold object, between hand and warm object.

Discussion of temperature receptors. Demonstration of presence of heat and cold receptors in skin.

Discussion of other kinds of receptors—e.g., pressure, light, sound; relate stimuli to forms of energy.

Responses of animals, plants, to light.

NOTE C: *Introduction to Chemical Reactions* (Grades 7–8)

ELEMENTS

Discussion of simplest type of materials, i.e., those consisting of one kind of atom only. Familiarization with the general properties of copper, iron, zinc, mercury and sulphur, by inspection and measurements (e.g. density) made on samples provided. Chemical symbols, and atomic arrangements by use of models. Idea of forces between atoms holding matter together, and that the forces depend on the atoms involved. Melting points measured (S), approximately measured (Zn), and given (remainder). Boiling points given and related to inter-atomic forces.

REACTIONS BETWEEN ELEMENTS TO FORM COMPOUNDS

When elements react, a compound is produced in which the two kinds of atoms are re-arranged to form a new pattern or lattice. Energy associated with reaction depends on: (a) forces holding atoms of elements together (stability, energy content), (b) forces holding atoms of the product together (stability, energy content). If energy is released, it may become obvious as heat. Experiments with Fe+S, Zn+S, Cu+S, Hg+S. Effect of temperature and state of elements (solid piece, powder, liquid) on the reaction.

Discussion of the differences between mixtures (e.g., iron filings and sulphur) before reaction and the compounds produced by the reaction. Models to show atomic arrangements of products and the 1:1 ratio of metal to sulphur atoms. Develop from such models the ideas of combining weights, constant composition and conservation of matter in chemical reactions.

Generalize to other chemical reactions, including (a) re-arrangement of atoms from reactants to products, (b) energy liberated or consumed depending on energy contents, (c) reason for slow or zero reaction at low temperatures (based on qualitative ideas of energy "humps").

OXYGEN

Resemblance to sulphur. Diatomic nature of O_2, pointing out the difference between the forces joining the two atoms of the molecule and the weak forces between molecules (typical of many gases and volatile liquids). Air contains oxygen (20 per cent): burning of substances in air (including rusting) is reaction between substance and oxygen, producing oxides (similar to sulphides). Experiments on formation and nature of oxides of copper, iron, zinc, mercury. Formulae, atomic arrangements and energy changes involved.

CARBON, HYDROGEN AND NITROGEN

Introduction on same lines as above. Note that nitrogen inert because of the strength of the N—N bond. Oxides of carbon and hydrogen (CO_2 and H_2O). Burning of organic matter (hydrocarbons) in air to give CO_2 and H_2O. NOTE: hydrocarbons [propane, methane] introduced as arrangements of C and H atoms, which re-arrange on oxidation in a way very similar to reactions of elements. Models, energy changes and nature of these oxides. Solution of CO_2 in H_2O to give carbonic acid which reacts with lime water (details later) to give an insoluble precipitate of calcium carbonate (details later). Characteristic test for CO_2 not given by other common gases—experiments to confirm if possible.

COMPOSITION OF AIR

Removal of oxygen by burning or rusting. Inert residue (N_2). Testing for CO_2 in air, breath, combustion products. Water vapour content by condensation, absorption. Mention of inert gases.

NOTE D: *Diffusion*

Diffusion is frequently introduced in elementary courses by experiments on the rapid spreading of odours in air, or on the spreading of dissolved colouring matter through a liquid. In both cases the effects observed are mainly due to convective transfer rather than diffusion. It is worth noting that, in the same courses, the parallel distinction between conductive and convective heat transfer in fluids is discussed much more carefully and the relative unimportance of the molecular process of heat transfer is emphasized. The slowness of diffusion should be carefully demonstrated and its inadequacy as a process for transporting materials over any great distances in animals and plants should be made clear, with emphasis on the relatively far greater importance of convection and flow in such transport.

Lightning Source UK Ltd.
Milton Keynes UK
UKHW010000210722
406167UK00001B/268